W9-AQH-425

BANTAM BOOKS

TORONTO ● NEW YORK ● LONDON ● SYDNEY ● AUCKLAND

SKYRAIDER

by
Robert F. Dorr

GROUND SUPPORT:

Jungle fires caused by Skyraider attacks on a suspected Viet Cong position. The Spad's ability to stay aloft for up to 12 hours, to fly low and slow, and carry up to 8,000 pounds of external ordnance plus four 20mm wing-mounted cannons made it one of the most effective aircraft of the Vietnam War in the ground support role.

AIR COMMANDOS:

Two 1st Air Commando Squadron A-1E Skyraiders returning to the dearming area at Pleiku Air Base after missions against the Viet Cong. Known as the ''Jungle Jims,'' the Air Commandos pioneered the US Air Force combat effort in Vietnam.

Many of the Air Commandos were veterans with two previous wars already under their belts. As a group they stood out as a loud, unruly, action-oriented band, who cared little for traditional discipline, and who disdained spit and polish. The Skyraider was their sort of aircraft; temperamental, spirited, and full of stamina.

CARRIER OPERATIONS:

Two US Navy A-1 Skyraiders prepare to take off from a carrier deck. Teamwork was the key to launch-and-recovery operations with the ordnancemen (inset left) and the landing signals officer (inset right) playing major roles. The Skyraider owed its existence to the Navy, which had commissioned the plane as a carrier-based bomber shortly after D-Day 1944. Over 20 years later this big, sturdy, but technologically outmoded, aircraft was still repaying the faith of the Navy planners.

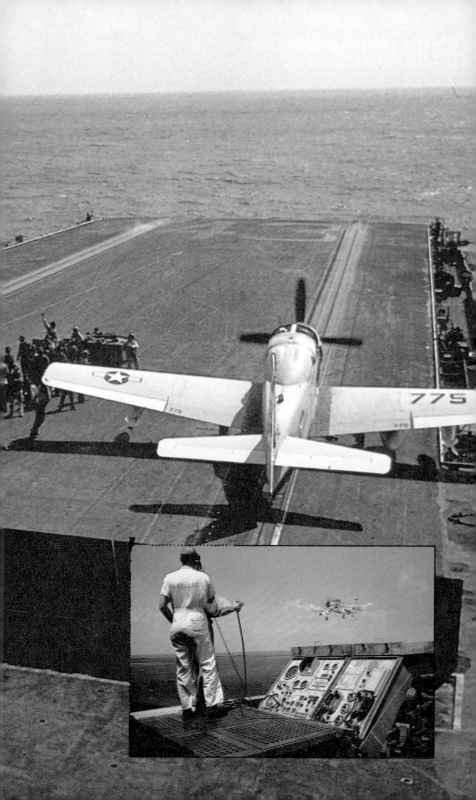

THE BLUE ROOM:

A US Air Force A-1E Skyraider heads towards a target. The tint of the rear canopy hood gave rise to the term "Blue Room" for the space behind the pilot. It was spacious enough to be used as an unofficial cargo bay by pilots shipping liquor and furniture. In some later versions the Blue Room housed electronic countermeasures operators and their equipment.

SPECIAL OPERATIONS:
An A-1G Skyraider climbs out of Nakhon Phanom in 1969. It was from this base in northern Thailand that special operations squadrons, flying Skyraiders, launched clandestine operations against communist forces in Laos. At the height of the operations, when Washington was asserting that no American had been killed there, some 200 airmen had lost their lives in Laos. Many of them were Skyraider pilots.

EDITOR IN CHIEF: Ian Ballantine.
SERIES EDITORS: Richard Grant, Richard Ballantine.
MAPS: Peter Williams. STUDIO: Kim Williams.
PRODUCED BY: The Up & Coming Publishing Company, Bearsville, New York.

SKYRAIDER
THE ILLUSTRATED HISTORY OF THE VIETNAM WAR
A Bantam Book/ July 1988

ACKNOWLEDGMENTS
While any mistakes in this volume are the fault of the author, Skyraider
would have been impossible without the generous assistance of many who
helped. Of particular importance were the contributions by James H.
Doolittle, 3rd and Norman Taylor.
I also want to thank Hal Andrews, Alexander D. Bache, Cliff Berry,
Ted Bronson, Eugene Deatrick, Mike Dugan, Jim Egbert, Doug Francis,
Harry Gann, Perrin Gower, Clay Johansson, Hubert G. King, Jr.,
David W. Menard, Peter Mersky, Robert C. Mikesh, R. J. Mills, Jr.,
Nguyen Cao Nguyen, David Ostrowski, Rosario Rausa, Bob Russell,
Jim Seith, "Deep Throat," and Charles Vasiliadis.
The views expressed in this book are the author's and do not necessarily
reflect those of the Department of State or of the United States Air Force.

The cutaway diagram on pages 86 and 87 is reproduced by permission of
Pilot Press Ltd.

Library of Congress Cataloging-in-Publication Data

Dorr, Robert F.
Skyraider.

(The Illustrated history of the Vietnam War)
1. Vietnamese Conflict, 1961–1975—Aerial operations.
2. Skyraider (Attack plane)   I. Title.   II. Series.
DS55.8.D668   1988   959.704'348   88-6164
ISBN 0-553-34548-6

Published simultaneously in the United States and Canada

PRINTED IN THE UNITED STATES OF AMERICA

CW 0   9   8   7   6   5   4   3   2   1

Contents

Air war in Shangri-la

The VNAF Buildup

THE FOUR A-1H Skyraiders bored through the clinging wet murk. Raindrops spattered like bullets into their windshields. The thunderstorm had come unexpectedly to the narrow South Vietnamese valleys along the Cambodian border.

It was May 1964 and Captain Al Bache felt a clammy dread inside. Suddenly it was dark, as black as Bache could remember, not just dusky dark but damned dark. With no horizon to look at, his aircraft vibrating violently enough to make his stomach heave, and barely able to see the Skyraider above and behind him, Captain Bache wasn't sure what scared him most—the weather, the Viet Cong in the rainlashed valleys below, or the pilot of that Skyraider.

As the US Air Force advisor to South Vietnam's 514th Fighter Squadron, Al Bache was number two in a four-ship formation. Before this mission, Bache had gotten a sharp warning.

The Vietnamese pilot of aircraft number three might be disloyal, he'd been told—a threat.

An hour earlier, the four Skyraiders had come hurling down out of the clouds, in a place where visibility was better, to drop bombs on a Viet Cong emplacement. They had done a lot of damage, Bache thought. His Skyraider might not be the prettiest thing in the sky, but it could tote six tons of bombs and rockets, and the Cong had learned to dive for cover when they saw it coming. The Skyraider, or Spad as some called it, was one doggoned good airplane in Bache's opinion, but you had to know what the rudder was for or you were in deep trouble.

Al's 514th Vietnamese squadron at Bien Hoa, commanded by Lieutenant Colonel Vo Van Si, had some real hot-rock pilots. Some had been flying since

17

Arming the button —A Vietnamese armorer checks the fuse on a bomb being loaded aboard a VNAF Spad. A mechanical tractor, known as an HLU-196, was used to lift the 250-pound bombs up to the wing pylons.

the early fifties alongside the French and had logged 3,000 hours in prop-driven warplanes. These were courageous and dedicated men. The warning to watch out for the pilot in Skyraider number three had seemed odd. There was political intrigue in this place, Bache realized, perhaps not unfitting for a Vietnam that in 1964 still seemed to Americans a faraway and exotic land with the flavor of Shangrila, the fictitious Asian hideaway of James Hilton's novel *Lost Horizon.*

Number Three was suspected of sympathies with the Viet Cong or with one of the Saigon factions that were forever plotting to overthrow the government of the day. A pilot had been lost a few weeks earlier. Number Three had been wingman. He was suspected of shooting down his own flight leader.

In the dark without any navigational aids, the Vietnamese pilots were flying by the seat of their pants—on the deck with no lights, skirting treetops, lightning flashing around them. Over the radio Number Three proclaimed that they would soon arrive at Bien Hoa.

Sensing the bulk of Number Three's aircraft looming in the murk behind him with its four 20mm cannons, Al Bache could not see how the man knew. He wondered if he was being buttered up for the slaughter. "No problem, *daewi* (captain). We make right turn now, okay?" There was further chatter in French, the language often used by the Vietnamese pilots.

"Either I'm about to get home free or I'm about to get blasted out of the sky," Bache told himself.

The formation wheeled into a right turn. The clouds broke. Suddenly revealed, bare in front of them, was the main runway at Bien Hoa, basking in the first sunshine Captain Bache had seen all day.

Demonstrating that he knew what the rudder was for, the captain used his rudder pedal, applied aileron, and took the bulky Skyraider into a turn to align itself for landing. It was plain as the nose on his face that he'd gotten a bum warning from Intel; if Number Three had intended to shoot him down it would have happened out in the storm-swept boondocks, not over home base. The Intel people needed their heads examined.

"You look good, *daewi.* No problem at all." On final approach, Bache came over runway's end,

Air war in Shangri-la

FINGER ON THE BUTTON:
Jets might soar in the stratosphere but Skyraiders fought down in the bushes where the war was. This A-1E Skyraider bears Vietnamese markings but the finger on the button despatching the 250-pound bomb into a Viet Cong jungle emplacement belongs to a US Air Force pilot.

Air war in Shangri-la

LOW-LEVEL ENTRY: An A-1 Skyraider is pulled by an aircraft tow tractor through downtown Saigon at midnight as a convoy makes its way from the waterfront to Tan Son Nhut airfield in 1965. By then the conflict had escalated sufficiently for the A-1s to require armed and wary guards—a sharp contrast to the arrival of the first A-1s in 1960, which were towed through the streets in an almost carnival atmosphere.

chopped power, and made a perfect landing. A few days later, on another mission against Viet Cong troops in bad weather, the suspect proved himself by spending 45 minutes loitering in the midst of enemy gunfire taking battle damage and heavy risk to help friendly ground forces.

They were brave men, flying the Skyraider, and theirs was one of the least publicized but most remarkable airplanes ever to serve in the Southeast Asia conflict.

WITH ITS HUGE, four-bladed propeller hanging out front and a tail wheel in back, the Skyraider was less an airplane than a collection of heavy iron; a

relic of the piston-engine prop age surviving, comfortably, in the jet age.

Its big Wright R-3350 piston engine smoked, belched, and wheezed, and was notorious for dripping oil, and then dripping more oil. This wasn't a leak, exactly, more like a programmed drip. A dirty flight suit was the Skyraider pilots' unofficial badge of office. The joke was, if Charlie didn't get you, you'd die by slipping on one of the oil slicks on any flight line where Skyraiders were parked. One pilot likened flying the Skyraider to playing the organ. "It had a lot of controls and pedals."

That 18-cylinder radial piston-driven R-3350 Cyclone was the biggest and most powerful engine

EARLY BIRDS:
The nucleus of
the VNAF's
Skyraider crews
were pilots who
had flown with
the French in
the early Fifties.
Unlike their
American
counterparts,
these
Vietnamese
pilots could
never look
forward to the
knowledge that
they would
rotate home
after one year.
For the VNAF
pilots the war
was never
finished.

ever put in a single-engine prop aircraft. It had to be, to pull the Skyraider through the air at gross weights of 26,000 pounds or more. Rated at 2,700 horsepower, the engine was the same as that used in the DC-7C airliner and men were very aware that everything about it spelled "big." By the early 1960s, the Navy, which had first commissioned the Skyraider, had a cadre of old salts who'd been turning wrenches on this engine for two decades. Some had risen to chief petty officer status; many knew more about the big Wright than the pilots who flew the airplane. When it came time to train the Vietnamese pilots, these chiefs were to prove indispensable.

A Skyraider flight line looked, and sounded, like World War II—which many of its pilots, in those early days of Vietnam, remembered well.

Designed at the end of World War II (though it never was used in that conflict), the Spad was known endearingly as a product of the Douglas Iron Works. In fact, Douglas's Ed Heinemann had designed a sturdy and effective warplane. A taildragger, 38 feet and 10 inches long, with a 50-foot wingspan, the Skyraider was so big that you could stand under it and look up at it. With a maximum speed of 310 knots, service ceiling of 27,000 feet, and a range of 1,100 nautical miles, the Skyraider could carry not only four 20mm cannons (with 150 rounds each) but up to 12,000 pounds of napalm, bombs, or rockets. Very simply, the Skyraider was the undisputed world champion at carrying ordnance. One typical load of 11,944 pounds on a combat mission included three 2,000-pound bombs, six 500-pounders, and six 250-pounders on its 15 wing stations.

Statistics alone do not tell the story. The Skyraider was tough as a tin can. It had a reputation for taking enemy fire again and again without going down. One returned from a mission with one hundred and eighteen 7.62mm bullet holes in its broad, sturdy wing. In the pressurized "wet" wing of a jet aircraft, just one such hit would have been fatal.

The Skyraider had the fuel capacity to loiter over a Viet Cong force for an hour or more (while jets quickly gulped their fuel and had to leave). Jet aircraft had become so complex that they depended on everything from trouble-prone transistors to a steady flow of costly parts. The Skyraider, in contrast, could be and often was put into the air with what pilots described as spit, prayer, and baling wire. Although the Skyraider did require maintenance, in contrast to jets, the venerable Spad was a joy to keep in working order. It was a different sort of flying; an F-104 pilot who volunteered to instruct the Vietnamese in Skyraiders explained, "I want to fly low enough so I can see people down on the ground."

FLYING COFFIN:
VNAF pilots at Bien Hoa in 1960 were flying the rapidly aging Grumman F8F Bearcat fighter. Twenty-eight of them had been handed over by the French, but had proved difficult to service. VNAF maintenance expert Nguyen Cao Nguyen's view was that it was a "flying coffin." Consequently the VNAF were delighted to receive new Skyraiders.

Air war in Shangri-la

FIRST IN:
Lt. Ken Moranville arrived at Bien Hoa in September 1960 to train Vietnamese pilots to fly the Skyraider. He was the first American naval officer in action in Southeast Asia. As Moranville quickly discovered, American advisors required diplomatic as well as military skills if they were to avoid becoming enmeshed in the political intrigues that were a frequent aspect of VNAF affairs.

DWIGHT D. EISENHOWER was president and Vietnam was a small, faraway war when the decision was made to beef up Saigon's air arm with surplus Skyraiders. Even in 1960, when it would never have occurred to a generation of innocent Americans to question a firm stand against communism, the idea of building up the Vietnamese Air Force (VNAF) was controversial. After all, Hanoi had no air force, nor was there the threat of a hostile air force being created. (Hanoi's own aerial buildup was to come later.) Decision makers had to show that, in bolstering Saigon's flying arm, they were not triggering a new arms race in the region. Congress had to be satisfied that whatever move was made next, it would not be provocative.

The Skyraider could be billed as a safe choice: It was old with a propeller up front. Its effect on VNAF fighting capability could be described to Congress as modest, indeed inconsequential.

Yet VNAF officers could be assured that they were receiving a potent weapon. The Skyraider could be "sold" as a first-line attack aircraft, still on active service with the US Navy while the F-80 Shooting Star, which was available to those Vietnamese pilots who wanted jets, had been long since retired.

The first six Skyraiders for the VNAF (Vietnamese Air Force) were shipped aboard a former US Navy jeep carrier, now employed as a merchantman, and arrived in Vietnam in September 1960. The old carrier came steaming up the Saigon River in full view of the Viet Cong on the city's outskirts, half the population of the capital, and the affluent crowd who watched the war from the rooftop terrace restaurant at the Caravelle Hotel. The ship docked at the foot of Rue Catinat, the road of revelry known in later years as Tu Do Street, and the massive Skyraiders, looking like flying tanks, were towed through the streets in the dead of night and down a country road to Bien Hoa. Twenty-five more Skyraiders for the VNAF arrived in similar fashion by May 1961.

The arrival of the Skyraiders was firm evidence of a US commitment to South Vietnam, a commitment cemented in a total absence of controversy late in the Eisenhower years. Saigon received funds and equipment. Thought was also given to sending American servicemen as advisors. In the wake of

Young veteran —Lt. Duy Chanh, a pilot with the 514th Fighter Bomber Squadron, VNAF, prepares to take off from Bien Hoa Air Base in November 1963. His Spad carried VNAF markings, but his flying helmet still carried the USAF emblem.

Air war in Shangri-la

AIR STRIKE: An A-1 Skyraider begins a bombing pass against a suspected Viet Cong position in January 1965. Americans who "advised" the VNAF were required to have a Vietnamese with them if they flew a combat mission. The rule was mostly cosmetic and, even before the restriction was lifted in 1965, it was often an American who guided the Skyraider over the quiltwork landscape of rubber plantations and paddy fields to attack a target.

Early consignment —With their wings folded, US Navy Skyraiders crowd the deck of the *Core* as it berths in Saigon harbor in 1965 amid strict security. The *Core* could carry up to 70 warplanes.

France's withdrawal from Indochina, the war against communist insurgents in South Vietnam was small, distant, even romantic in the eyes of Americans. Providing help to a friendly air force was a small step, hardly likely to arouse much dissent. In 1960, candidates Nixon and Kennedy argued over who would do more to fight communism if elected. Both favored support for South Vietnam.

Until the arrival of the Skyraiders, the VNAF had carried out its aerial conflict against the insurgents using the much-loved but elderly Grumman F8F Bearcat. Much-loved, that is, by pilots; maintenance expert Nguyen Cao Nguyen called it a "flying coffin." The Bearcat was a legacy left by the French; Skyraiders became the first warplanes brought to Vietnam by the Americans.

Six hand-picked Vietnamese pilots travelled stateside to "learn Skyraider," as they put it, with the US Navy's Aviation Training Unit 301(ATU-301) at the NAS (Naval Air Station) Corpus Christi, Texas. They formed the nucleus of the VNAF's Skyraider force at Bien Hoa. It was at this air base north of Saigon that Lieutenant Kenneth E. Moranville was sent to oversee the training effort, with help from a handful of chiefs who knew the R-3350 engine inside and out. Moranville was to become the first US naval officer to see action in Vietnam.

When Ken Moranville arrived at Bien Hoa in September 1960, his half-dozen VNAF Skyraiders were in " like new" condition but were missing key items, including normal seat parachutes. The lieutenant set up a training program for his Vietnamese charges and began flying on their wing in a Bearcat or Skyraider to watch their progress. The VNAF was flying "on call" missions against Viet Cong guerrillas, often guided by an L-19 spotter plane, and although Americans were forbidden from flying in combat, Moranville, an activist, could not help becoming deeply immersed in the events around him.

A sidelight of the Skyraider story is the frequency with which questions arose about the loyalties of a few VNAF pilots. On November 11, 1960, a coup was unleashed against President Ngo Dinh Diem by rebel paratroopers. At Bien Hoa, VNAF pilots scrambled into the air intending to use their Bearcats and Skyraiders to bomb the coup leaders.

The planes circled over the rebels' heads with full bomb loads and intimidated them into surrendering. There was no bloodshed.

On a typical antiguerrilla mission, Moranville's pilots of the Bien Hoa-based VNAF 1st Fighter Squadron would take off carrying four 500-pound bombs and two canisters of nineteen 2.75-inch folding fin aircraft rockets (FFAR). On discovering a group of Viet Cong moving through the brush, the spotter L-19 would mark the enemy with smoke grenades and direct the Skyraiders by radio.

In those early days, Bearcats and Skyraiders flew side by side. In one tragic accident, a Bearcat was shot down at treetop level, apparently by a VC wielding a World War II bazooka. The pilot was killed. Nearly all of the pilots in the squadron from 1960 to 1962, including all six who had trained in Texas, died in the war.

It fell upon Ken Moranville's shoulders to check out one pilot new to the Skyraider who did survive, Nguyen Cao Ky. Moranville saw Ky, a VNAF transport squadron CO (commanding officer), as a charismatic figure and a future leader. Ky found the Skyraider more attuned to his flamboyant style than the multi-engine airplanes he'd been flying and was pleased when Moranville praised his natural "feel" at the controls.

Personal insignia —The nose cowling of an A-1H Skyraider of the Vietnamese Air Force (VNAF) painted with a tiger's head— the insignia most commonly associated with Air Marshal Nguyen Cao Ky.

The Skyraider was something of a challenge for the VNAF's mechanics. Generous in providing the airplanes, the US had been niggardly with spare parts and maintenance manuals. Energetic in training Vietnamese pilots, the Americans had not paid nearly enough attention to the ground crewmen, who possessed limited maintenance skills and were sorely underequipped. Still, the Skyraider was a better aircraft under the circumstances than any jet would have been.

The Viet Cong could hardly fail to notice the Skyraider. Many of the better VNAF pilots attacked at altitudes as low as 500 feet (one came back from a mission with the branch of a tree mashed inside the huge open cowling) and a Skyraider at 500 feet with all guns blazing was an impressive sight. The VNAF was becoming more and more proficient with the Skyraider during the Kennedy years, when the US role in Vietnam was increasing gradually.

At the beginning of 1962, the Vietnamese combat

CHANGING COLORS

AS THE VIETNAM conflict changed in character from a low-intensity counter-insurgency operation to a full-scale war, so did the appearance of the Skyraiders flown by the VNAF. The early airplanes, like this AD-6 (A-1H) Skyraider (top) of the VNAF's 1st Fighter Squadron photographed at Bien Hoa in October 1962, arrived in pristine condition painted in a shade of gloss gray-white similar to that favored by the US Navy. But that soon changed.

The A1-H (center) is devoid of national insignia, often a sign of involvement in clandestine operations. Instead it is draped in the black paint scheme of the VNAF's 83rd Special Operations Group, which participated in operations in North Vietnam and Laos.

More common among VNAF Skyraiders was the use of subdued national insignia as seen (bottom) on this Spad of the 518th taxiing at Tan Son Nhut in July 1971. Subdued insignia made it difficult for the enemy to spot and record individual A-1s, making it harder for them to gather intelligence about their successes and failures in shooting VNAF Skyraiders.

inventory consisted of 22 A-1 Skyraiders. Thirty T-28s arrived in March. As its strength grew, the VNAF was able to mount a 50-plane raid on a Viet Cong redoubt in the Central Highlands on May 27, 1962. Sorties flown by the Skyraiders went up from 150 in January to 390 in June.

Internal strife remained a problem. On February 26, 1963, two disgruntled VNAF pilots bombed Ngo Dinh Diem's palace in Saigon. Other Skyraiders attempted to intercept them. One of the renegades was shot down by ground fire and was killed while the other hightailed it to Cambodia where he crashed his Spad. Diem was so angered by this latest challenge to presidential authority that he grounded the entire VNAF for a time.

The VNAF's first Skyraider squadron, called the 1st in Moranville's time, the 514th in Bache's (it was redesignated the 514th Fighter Squadron on January 1, 1963) was only the beginning for Saigon's Skyraider force. Half a dozen VNAF squadrons eventually acquired Skyraiders.

In theory the US Air Force, not the Navy, was responsible for training VNAF pilots. This worked fine as long as Saigon's pilots were flying Air Force planes like the T-28 and B-26 but the Skyraider had always been exclusively a naval warplane and there was no one in shade 84 blue who knew how to fly it. While the Air Force quickly sought to acquire Skyraiders, three young naval officers were sent to Bien Hoa to continue the training effort.

Ted Bronson, Tom Conway, and Doug Francis were assigned to the 514th Squadron at Bien Hoa from April to October 1963. Their orders were issued directly by the Chief of Naval Operations rather than, as normal, the Navy's bureau of personnel. They were told to get the expanding VNAF Skyraider force into shape and, above all, to stay out of politics. Bronson remembers that their students seemed eager; one reproduced a color diagram of the Skyraider electrical system on a blackboard with colored chalk.

Colonel Huynh Huu Hien, chief of the VNAF in 1963, heaped praise on the Navy Skyraider instructors. At this juncture, their student body consisted of two kinds—T-28 pilots transitioning to the Skyraider, and day-qualified Skyraider pilots learning night work. Training and the dropping of bombs on

Going solo —A VNAF pilot of the 514th gives his crew chief the thumbs-up to indicate that he is ready for take off. VNAF pilots were first trained by the Navy and later by the Air Commandos, but after 1965 Saigon's air force developed the capability to provide its own training.

the Viet Cong proceeded side by side, as did the endless palace intrigue of Saigon in the early 1960s. Under stringent restrictions about any discussion of the political situation in Vietnam, Ted Bronson was asked his opinion of the controversial Madame Nhu, sister-in-law of President Diem and considered to be the most powerful woman in Saigon.

"Who?" Bronson responded.

Later in the year violence removed Diem and John F. Kennedy from the scene. The Saigon government underwent a series of changes. Nguyen Cao Ky became chief of the VNAF.

When the Air Force's Al Bache, an F-104 pilot who had converted to the prop job with ATU-301 at Corpus, arrived at Bien Hoa to join the 514th in March 1964, a further VNAF squadron, the 518th under Lieutenant Colonel Quoc, was being formed for long-distance, low-level work. The 518th was also

FULL LOAD: Bien Hoa 1963, and the 514th Squadron of the VNAF proudly layout their impressive array of weapons that their recently acquired Skyraiders can carry. Shown here are cannons, rocket pods, 5-inch rockets, 250- and 500-pound bombs, and mine dispensers. Machine gun belts (center) display the squadron's number.

the unit with which Air Force chief Ky was most closely associated. Much talk had been heard about taking the war to North Vietnam and the 518th's preparations with its Skyraiders hinted at widening hostilities to come.

More Americans trickled into the country. The US Air Force's 34th Tactical Group under Colonel Bill Bethea set up shop at Bien Hoa. Its people were "those wild guys in bush hats," as one observer called them. They were Air Commandos, supposedly the elite, and they'd already been in-country flying against the Viet Cong with their T-28s and B-26s.

Now they had Skyraiders. Until now, the Skyraider had belonged only to Vietnamese squadrons with American advisors. The Air Commandos of the 34th put American markings on the Spad and, not content with the familiar single-seat A-1H, introduced the A-1E with side-by-side seats up front.

Wrong forecast —Robert S. McNamara, Secretary of Defense, 1961-68. In 1964 he predicted the withdrawal of US airmen from South Vietnam would happen within months. It took another 8 years.

In due course, the 34th Group at Bien Hoa was to include two key American Spad squadrons—the First Air Commando and the 602nd Fighter Squadron (Commando). Later in the war, with a major change to nomenclature, both were to become known as Special Operations Squadrons, or SOS.

The war was about to lose its adventuresome *Terry and the Pirates* flavor. The two Americans with the VNAF's 514th, Bache and pilot/maintenance expert Joe Saureissig, may have been the last Americans in Nam to experience that sense of adventure. Flying over the flat paddy fields in the south with your canopy open and the slipstream rushing in, taking care to avoid exhaust fumes from flying too slow, accompanied by the roar of the R-3350, and the solid feeling of a shoulder holster packed with a .38 Combat Master, there was that sense of living and working with basics. The thought came to Bache that time had halted. It could have been 20 years earlier.

Nothing stayed small, however. Including the VNAF. The 516th Fighter Squadron at Da Nang converted from T-28s to Skyraiders in May 1964. The 520th and 522nd at Bien Hoa and Tan Son Nhut soon followed. Later, a 524th squadron was formed at Nha Trang.

The Kennedy era faded; the Johnson period took hold. There was a brief respite when it looked like the war was going to end and the few American advisors would be able to pull out. On a visit to Saigon in May 1964, Defense Secretary Robert S. McNamara reiterated a familiar theme, saying that all US airmen should be out of combat within a matter of months.

The Americans were told to limit their activities to providing genuine training only, an order that was almost impossible to obey while submerged in coups and combat. A withdrawal of US personnel was not going to start, said McNamara, it was going to "continue." The VNAF was to receive additional A-1H Skyraiders and would take over all functions performed by the Air Commandos. There were to be several such pronouncements from McNamara, and an 0-1 Birddog squadron was actually removed from South Vietnam, but the trend was decidedly not toward a US disengagement.

Instead, the US role grew. The A-1 Skyraider was

still a US Navy aircraft, although the US Air Force was beginning to operate its own.

At NAS Moffett Field, California, Lieutenant Doug Francis—back now, from Bien Hoa--was roped into a hush-hush project.

A Navy civilian from "some special lab in Jacksonville" oversaw things while Francis flew around in a Skyraider with a peculiar cargo slung under the wings, two tanks built by a firm called Agronomics in Santa Clara, California. The tanks had propellers up front and spray bars on the back. "I thought they were intended for nerve gas," Francis said.

The project was so closely guarded that Francis had no idea why the Skyraider was ultimately rejected in favor of the C-123 transport for the secret "crop dusting" program. He was the only pilot in a hush-hush sidelight of Skyraider history that didn't seem important now that the war was ending. It was 1964. In yet another of his "light at the end of the tunnel" pronouncements Defense Secretary McNamara had said that 1,000 of the 15,000 Americans in Vietnam would be withdrawn by the end of the year. Doug Francis had never heard of Agent Orange, the defoliant that would become notorious for leaving behind a trail of genetic damage that could afflict immediate descendants of those who came into contact with it.

TURNAROUND: **The refuelling and re-arming flight line at Tan Son Nhut airbase. Once President Nixon's policy of Vietnamization came into effect in 1970 the VNAF rapidly became proficient at fast turnarounds. By December 1972, the VNAF was the fourth largest air force in the world with 65 squadrons.**

A Spad for Jungle Jim

CHAPTER

2

Air Commandos

IF THE VNAF had been the first service to use the Skyraider in Southeast Asia, the US Air Force could claim that it was not very far behind. In fact, the Air Force took over from the Navy the entire job of training Vietnamese pilots.

In the early 1960s, the Air Force's special warfare experts were drawn together at Hurlburt Field near Fort Walton Beach, Florida, and were known as Air Commandos. Fighter pilots and crusty NCOs and airmen, many with two previous wars under their belts, they were a loud, unruly, and action-oriented band of brothers who cared little for traditional discipline and who disdained spit and polish. They took their irreverent manner and fighting spirit from the World War II air commandos of Colonel "Flip" Cochran of the China-Burma-India theater, who had been role model for a *Terry and the Pirates* comic-strip adventure character. Like Cochran, they wore an Aussie-style bush hat. Like the Army Special Forces' better-known green beret, it distinguished them as men of an elite force.

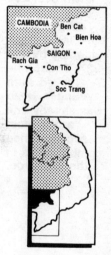

In October 1961, President Kennedy authorized deployment of the Air Commandos to the battle zone to train Saigon's airmen in the T-28. Soon, a B-26 detachment followed. The Air Commandos went to Vietnam in a contingent known as "Jungle Jim," their operation in-country was code-named "Farm Gate." On November 4, 1961, they arrived at Bien Hoa with 151 officers and men, eight T-28s, four C-47s, and four B-26s.

The Air Commandos came to a land of parched heat and choking red dust in the dry season, mud and thunderstorms in the wet. Frothy white clouds made flying hazardous all year around in the deep

37

Combat vet —It took more than a bush hat to make an Air Commando. Air Force Academy graduate Captain Richard G. Head had flown over 200 combat missions and survived a crash landing by age 27. Though he looked even younger, Head was already one of the most accomplished combat pilots in the Air Force.

valleys and sheer ridgelines of much of the country. They came to train Vietnamese allies—not the seasoned pilots who'd flown with the French but a new generation of fledglings with less motivation, less ability, and little English. But the Air Commandos also came to fight. There was, in them, a little of the spirit of the Flying Tigers, of Cochran, of *Terry and the Pirates*, of every brash young American who'd ever hauled himself off to Asia for a small dirty war in an exotic setting.

One Air Commando had gotten the assignment by staring his personnel handler in the face and taunting, "Are you gonna tell me that as a young fighter pilot in the United States Air Force I can't volunteer to go off and fight in the only war we've got?"

The rest of the Air Force might have its century series jets ranging from the F-100 Super Sabre to the F-105 Thunderchief, as well as the new F-4 Phantom, but in these early days of conflict a prop job was the way to get into action. A handful of RF-101C Voodoo reconnaissance jets were flying risky photo-gathering missions over Vietnam and Laos but none of the other jet fighters had yet joined the struggle. Most of the Air Commandos were men who'd flown jets in the past and had switched to props in order to have a chance to fight.

The Americans were flying in combat, but no one would say so for public consumption. To preserve the fiction that they were merely advisors, the rules demanded a Vietnamese on board the aircraft during any combat mission. Many of the younger VNAF fliers became little more than unwanted passengers on a combat mission where the American half of the crew did all of the flying and fighting.

As they searched the Vietnamese coast for seaborne infiltrators and flew direct support for ARVN troops fighting the VC, Farm Gate's airmen came to understand that their T-28s, and in particular the B-26s, were not right for the severe climatic demands, the poor maintenance, and the persistent problems, such as fuel contamination, unique to this conflict. They cast an envious eye at their Navy brethren who were instructing the Vietnamese in the Skyraider—a job they were soon to take over. Structural fatigue in the T-28s and B-26s was a "health hazard" of near scandalous proportions. Congressmen began to hear that our boys had been

sent to Vietnam to fly old, decrepit airplanes that fell apart in midair.

This was an exaggeration, but in August 1963 a B-26 suffered a wing failure during a combat mission, killing two Americans and the requisite Vietnamese crewman. A short time later, another B-26 was lost when its wings came apart in midair and a T-28, too, went down due to a mechanical failure. The widow of an Air Force captain released to a national magazine his letters telling of his premonition that he would die because of the poor maintenance and structural flaws of this aircraft.

A fix was eventually found for the B-26s; wing racks loaded with 750-pound bombs were discovered to be the cause of overstressing, which resulted in main spar cracks when the aircraft was taxiing. The B-26s were withdrawn by early 1964 and the "Cap-

BEFORE THE SPAD

The venerable T-28 trainer (left) and the Korean War vintage Douglas B-26 Invader (right) were the first planes flown in Vietnam by the "Jungle Jim" contingent of Air Commandos, which arrived in-country in November 1961 to train Vietnamese pilots and fly alongside them on combat missions.

Both planes proved unsuitable for the severe climatic conditions, both required frequent maintenance, which was in short supply, and the B-26 was prone to

tain Swank letters" in *Look* magazine almost certainly boosted the Air Force decision to re-equip Farm Gate's Air Commandos with the A-1 Skyraider.

The VNAF had received only the single-seat Skyraider, the A-1H. Following on the heels of the 34th Tactical Group, the 1st Air Commando Squadron, known as the Hobo Squadron, received the A-1E version, that had been originally designed for the Navy, with an oversized cockpit allowing side-by-side seating for a pilot and navigator up front and two more seats aft for electronics equipment operators.

structural fatigue. Two B-26s suffered wing-failures, killing their crews. Eventually the fault was diagnosed: The wing racks for 750-pound bombs were becoming overstressed when the aircraft was taxiing and this in turn was causing main spar cracks. Both the B-26 and the T-28 were withdrawn from Vietnam service and by early 1964 the Air Commandos were flying Skyraiders.

The Air Commandos retained the two seats up front, primarily for the required Vietnamese crewman. The aft section, called the "Blue Room" because of its tinted Plexiglas canopy, was gutted of the third and fourth seats and became a handy "crawlspace" for unusual cargoes. One pilot used the space to carry rattan furniture from the Philippines; another returned from a Saigon visit with several cases of a dry white wine from the commissary. A bulletproof door behind the cockpit seats was regarded as armor to protect the pilot from the rear. After a pilot went down on the beach at Soc Trang and perished because rescuers could enter the wreckage only through the Blue Room—and found the door wired shut—a warning was issued to keep it unlocked. The order was disregarded; unlocked, the door flapped noisily and was a nuisance.

Although in far better flying condition than the T-28s and B-26s—most had been completely overhauled and were pristine when they arrived in Vietnam—the Skyraider was *old.* Armorers at Bien Hoa realized that the A-1E, or "Maytag Washing Machine" as someone christened the aircraft, had carried numerous kinds of underwing ordnance over the years. Each time a new bomb or rocket was introduced, the Skyraider was rewired to carry it. One crew chief remembered finding some of the airplanes with up to 500 pounds of wire inside the wings."Nobody could remember which wires were connected to what. So we had no way to remove the excess, and our pilots paid a penalty in extra flying weight."

Communications were poor. Faulty bomb fuses caused a premature detonation of 500-pounders that killed a Hobo Squadron pilot near Rach-Gia in the Delta. The old 20mm cannons on the Skyraider were so worn out they sometimes exploded and threw shrapnel in all directions, on one occasion narrowly missing a pilot's head. For every one of the highly motivated VNAF pilots who kept logging extra combat hours and taking extra risks, there seemed to be two others who wanted to wear bright-colored

HOME BASE: The Air Commandos got their start in 1964 at Bien Hoa with the 34th Tactical Group, which soon encompassed the First Air Commando and 602nd Fighter Squadrons. Later in the war, these and other Skyraider outfits became known as Special Operations Squadrons and became part of the 14th Wing at Nha Trang.

scarves and chase women but were only too reluctant to fly. Few of the VNAF people spoke any English; almost none of the Americans knew Vietnamese or French. The Air Commandos were supposed to be helping a friendly ally to expand and improve his air force but at times they felt they were out there all alone, taking the brunt of a battle nobody else knew or cared about.

Major Charles ("Vas") Vasiliadis arrived at Bien Hoa in November 1964 to join the 1st Air Commando Squadron and promptly racked up the first of no fewer than 493 combat missions in the A-1E Skyraider. One day, leading his flight with the call sign Norm 61, Vas bombed a VC tunnel complex in a densely wooded area 8 miles west of the Ben Cat US Army Special Forces camp. A few days later, he was carrying 500-pounders against a VC-occupied village a mere 20 miles northwest of Bien Hoa.

On this mission, Major Vas forgot to throw a switch to shift from the Skyraider's external fuel tank to internal fuel. Pulling away from a bomb run, his Vietnamese passenger asleep beside him, he pulled full rudder to cope with the very strong torque characteristic of the Skyraider and was climbing over flat paddyfields when the big R-3350 engine began to sputter and groan. His passenger snapped

ALLIES:
A US pilot attached to the VNAF 514th Squadron and two Vietnamese pilots return from a combat mission. Once the Air Commandos had Skyraiders, they gradually took over the job of flying combat. Their original job of training VNAF pilots became less important after 1965 when Saigon's air force had the capability to provide its own training.

A Spad for Jungle Jim

awake, thought it was time to bail out, and started to climb over the side.

Vasiliadis had sharp memories of once finding a downed VNAF crewmate after the Viet Cong had castrated him, and didn't want his own crewman to suffer a similar fate in the enemy-controlled terrain below. At the same time, the major had to get control of his aircraft. He released the stick long enough to grab the Vietnamese and the Skyraider's nose plummeted downward. He released the Vietnamese long enough to grab the stick and the man tried to bail out again. "No, no, no!" Major Vas shrieked

above the sputtering of the engine and the roar of the airstream blasting into the open canopy. Rice paddies spun crazily in front of them as Vasiliadis belatedly remembered the fuel switch, flipped it, and felt the engine belch back to life. The Skyraider settled into a gentle climb. The Vietnamese nodded, grinned sheepishly, and sat back in his seat.

When the August 1964 Gulf of Tonkin incident signalled a much-increased US role in the war, a second Air Commando squadron moved into Bien Hoa with Skyraiders. The 602nd Fighter Squadron (Commando) was headed by Lieutenant Colonel Andy

GOOD PRACTICE:
Checking the fuses of 250-pound general purpose (GP) bombs became routine for Maj. Charles C. Vasiliadis of the 1st Air Commando Squadron. Charlie Vas, as he was known, flew 493 combat missions in the Spad. In November 1965, this was more missions than any other Air Force pilot in Vietnam.

Chapman. The war was widening now, and the comforts of Hootch Row at Bien Hoa were strained by overcrowding. Some of the younger Vietnamese pilots, like their elders, had now become very proficient in the Skyraider. In addition to the 514th, 516th, and 518th VNAF squadrons, Nguyen Cao Ky now had an elite force of all-black Skyraiders with the 83rd Special Operations Group at Saigon's Tan Son Nhut air base. But as everything got bigger and better, the Air Commandos kept wondering if they would ever be able to fly into combat by themselves.

Every Air Commando had a story about some VNAF fledgling who didn't quite measure up, but it soon became clear that the majority of the younger, less motivated Vietnamese pilots were becoming skillful in the A-1 Skyraider. In the 1960-64 period, the name of the game was to get the Vietnamese to the point where they could defend themselves—only a few voices were calling for a wider war, for bombing of North Vietnam—and the VNAF Skyraider guys seemed to be doing it.

Part of the credit had to go to Nguyen Cao Ky, who became chief of staff of the air force from December 1963. The American press razzed Ky for appearing with his beautiful young wife in flashy matching flight coveralls, but his young pilots, sergeants, and enlisted troops lapped it up. They knew from the evidence that Ky was not only a showman, although showmanship was essential to his leadership style. They knew that Ky was ready to lead by example and that when it came time to fly into a hail of enemy gunfire, he would be at the head of the pack. It was true that one of his colleagues was being charitable in describing Ky as a *"very average"* pilot, but Ky was above all a superb officer and leader.

In those years just before the massive buildup that transformed Vietnam into an American war, the Skyraider became the bulwark of the Vietnamese Air Force and the backbone of the aerial effort against the Viet Cong insurgency. Despite the outdated 20mm cannons that desperately needed to be replaced, the A-1 Skyraider was in excellent condition (unlike the T-28 and B-26). Skyraider airframes had the potential for thousands of additional combat hours. Trained first by Navy men, later by Air Commandos, the VNAF pilots were becoming hot rocks.

As early as April 1963, the sole VNAF Skyraider

BOMB RUN:
Flown by an Air Commando, an A-1E Skyraider bombs targets in South Vietnam. Its 15 pylons could carry bombs from 250 to 1,000 pounds.

squadron at the time (the 1st, newly renamed 514th, Fighter Squadron) had flown 1,500 combat sorties against Viet Cong personnel and emplacements. By April 1964, more than 10,000 Skyraider sorties had been logged.

The Skyraider had become the principal attack aircraft of the VNAF. The big, burly prop-driven attack plane became a ubiquitous sight over the battlefield whenever ARVN (Army of Vietnam) and Viet Cong forces were pitted against each other. Skyraiders made the difference more than once when a friendly camp was beseiged and almost overrun by the Viet Cong. ARVN outposts and US Special Forces camps that would have fallen to the enemy were saved because the Skyraider could bring devastating ordnance to the scene, stay around for the fight, and if necessary fly and fight after dark.

VNAF Skyraiders were among the first aircraft to be camouflaged, a practice that became widespread by mid-1965. When the VNAF 83rd Special Operations Group was formed by Ky, with its 522nd Fighter Squadron as an elite unit with the expectation of special missions ahead, a variety of camouflage schemes were tried, including all black with national insignia deleted. Most VNAF Skyraiders simply shed their navy-style gray and white paint scheme in favor of the green, olive drab and tan paint design known to the US Air Force as "T.O. 1-1-4" or "Southeast Asia camouflage."

After the Gulf of Tonkin incident in August 1964, a major turning point in the war, came the beginning of the Rolling Thunder campaign against North Vietnam in March 1965. On March 2, 1965, in the first major strikes against North Vietnam, the A-1 Skyraider enjoyed a brief episode "up north." Al Bache went up north on that mission in one of the Air Commandos' A-1E airplanes. As Bache, Zack Haynes, and other US Air Force pilots dived on their assigned target, Nguyen Cao Ky led his own Skyraiders to another North Vietnamese target further inland, even though this had not been part of the plan. The war against the North had begun.

But the real turning point for the Air Commandos was the Easter announcement that they would no longer be required to carry a Vietnamese crewman while flying a combat mission. It was 1965 and it was becoming an American war.

Convert to props —Lt. Col. Hal Boyce, operations officer of the 34th Tactical Group, firing up his A-1E Skyraider for a mission from Bien Hoa. An experienced jet pilot, Boyce was thrown into flying the prop-driven Spad by the demands of war.

A Spad for Jungle Jim

HALF A WING AND A PRAYER: On September 1, 1966, Lee Minnick of the 602nd was covering a rescue in the Gulf when North Vietnamese shore batteries blew off half of the right wing of airplane 132684. It says much for the Skyraider's stability and basic airworthiness that Minnick was able to coax the badly damaged Skyraider to a safe spot where he bailed out and was rescued.

49

The Tonkin Gulf Yacht Club

CHAPTER

3

Carrier-based operations

THE FIRST AMERICAN to die in the skies of North Vietnam was Richard C. Sather, pilot of an A-1H Skyraider shot down on August 5, 1964. Following torpedo boat attacks on US destroyers on August 2 and 4, President Lyndon Johnson decided to retaliate by ordering aircraft from the carriers *Ticonderoga* and *Constellation* to strike targets in North Vietnam. The two carriers' air wings flew 64 attack sorties, destroying more than half the North Vietnamese torpedo boat force and setting afire POL (petroleum, oil, and lubricant) supplies.

This was the Gulf of Tonkin incident, the first giant step toward expanding and Americanizing the war. It led to a congressional resolution widely understood to give Johnson a free hand. From the standpoint of Skyraider pilots and others aboard the carriers at sea, the incident provided a one-time-only opportunity to test their mettle against Hanoi's defenses, which at this time consisted mostly of antiaircraft guns—MiG jets and SAM missiles would come later—although more than a few men wondered why Secretary McNamara announced the targets while carrier planes were still en route to them.

North Vietnamese gunfire was sporadic and inaccurate. Several Skyraider pilots availed themselves of the second chance afforded by their plane's great fuel capacity, making second and third efforts to deliver their bombs accurately. For most, the flight into North Vietnam was quick, surgical, and

The Tonkin Gulf Yacht Club

THE SPAD AND THE SCOOTER: An AD Skyraider refuels an A-4 Skyhawk "Scooter" jet from its 300-gallon centerline fuel tank using the probe-and-drogue technique. Although overtaken by the larger land-based KC-130 tanker, which could refuel two aircraft simultaneously, the Skyraider was the only carrier-based aircraft capable of this role. Its ability to take on multiple tasks only added to its reputation as a versatile utility aircraft.

eventless. But included in the cost of the one-day raid was the capture of the first American prisoner of war, A-4C Skyhawk pilot Lieutenant (j.g.) Everett Alvarez, as well as the loss of Sather. The Skyraider, which had operated from carriers since the 1940s, proved itself well.

In the "Tonkin Gulf Yacht Club," as navymen dubbed their floating enterprise off the enemy's coast—the term belied the rigor and danger of carrier aviation—it was usually the jets that received praise and attention. As the war widened in 1965 and the US began sustained air operations over North Vietnam, press stories focused on action by the jets. The Skyraider was now the last prop-driven combat aircraft on carrier decks and was

surrounded by sleeker, fancier Phantoms,
Crusaders, and Skyhawks. Hardly anyone seemed
to notice that a big, sturdy attack aircraft with a
prop up front was carrying a considerable proportion
of the air war against Hanoi.

For the remainder of the war, one or more US
carriers operated from Yankee Station facing North
Vietnam and at least one carrier was always on
Dixie Station to cover missions over South Vietnam.
The 1965-68 Rolling Thunder campaign against
North Vietnam eclipsed the remainder of the
Skyraider's service life; by its end, there would be
no more A-1s operating from carrier decks. But no
other aircraft was ever quite so effective in carrying
heavy bomb loads, providing close air support—

The price
—Lt. James S.
Hardie examines
the bullet-ridden
fuselage of his
A-1. Hardie was
one of the
carrier pilots
who attacked
North
Vietnamese
installations on
August 5, 1964,
in retaliation for
the Gulf of
Tonkin incident.
Hardie's
Skyraider was
hit by enemy
gunfire but he
succeeded in
nursing the
plane home to
his carrier.

sometimes almost too close for comfort—and loitering in a target area in blatant defiance of the enemy's guns.

Skyraiders flew so many kinds of sorties that it was almost impossible to speak of a typical mission. A strike against a marshalling yard in North Vietnam routinely meant a three- to four-hour mission carrying six 500-pound Mark 82 bombs and thirty-eight 2.75-inch rockets on a "lo-hi-lo" profile in which the Skyraider started out at wavecap altitude and returned to low level once approaching the target. A close air support mission in South Vietnam often meant up to six or seven hours in the cockpit, much of it spent circling Viet Cong or NVA troops, delivering up to twelve 500-pound napalm tanks, and riddling the enemy with 20mm cannon fire.

There was absolutely no doubt that Skyraider operations were having an impact on the enemy's ability to wage war. Viet Cong prisoners when being interrogated rarely had the knowledge or the motive to talk about a particular item of American equipment. But the A-1, which became "Skyraider" in the Vietnamese language as well as the English, was known to even low-ranking enemy troopers. Captured documents showed that the VC and the North Vietnamese were impressed by the carrier-based warplane's ability to survive under fire while carrying out difficult missions.

And difficult these missions indeed were. The Skyraider had a spacious cockpit and the Navy's single-seat A-1H and A-1J enjoyed superb visibility. But the pilot had to begin with a gut-wrenching catapult launch, spend hours cranking his head in every direction looking for enemy action, make repeated passes over the target, and finally live through the disconcerting experience of trying to set down his heavy aircraft, possibly with battle damage, on a carrier deck that looked from the air no larger than a postage stamp. Missions in the jets were shorter and involved shorter durations of exposure to enemy fire. Jet or prop, naval aviators operating from carrier decks faced a formidable adversary in North Vietnam.

BEGINNING IN 1965, North Vietnam was defended not merely by guns (sometimes called antiaircraft artillery, or Triple-A) but by surface-to-air missiles (SAMs) and an increasing number of Soviet-supplied MiG fighters.

A pilot flying over the North could get hit by a 7.62mm rifle bullet, by a high-explosive 85mm shell from a gun guided by Fire Can radar, or by half a dozen sizes in between. Guns were dangerous at all altitudes but were especially lethal below 5,000 feet. The middle altitudes between 15,000 and 30,000 feet where US airmen once cruised with impunity became the province of the SAM, a fearful newcomer to the art of war. MiGs prowled the medium and higher altitudes, up to 40,000 feet.

Pilots learned that if you could spot the red burn of a SAM's sustainer engine or get warning that it was coming, you could outmaneuver it—but this lesson came slowly and the SAM never quite lost its aura of dread. SAMs that weren't spotted in time knocked down several Navy warplanes in mid and late 1965. In the Skyraider, though, it was always recognized that the MiG was even more dangerous.

With missiles, MiGs, and Triple-A to worry about, people were going to get shot down. There came into being an elaborate force with the sole purpose of rescuing downed pilots. Tankers to supply fuel, Iron Hand aircraft to attack SAM radars, the C-130 airborne command post, and Jolly Green Giant helicopters, all could be assembled into a massive search and rescue (SAR) armada to move in quickly and decisively when a rescue was needed. The Navy recognized early that such a force required a heavily armed escort capable of pinning down enemy troops while guiding Jolly Greens in for the pickup. The Skyraider was the obvious choice.

Lieutenant Commander Edward Greathouse was division leader of four Skyraiders sent from *Midway* on June 20, 1965, to cover the rescue of an F-105 pilot downed near Dien Bien Phu. Greathouse belonged to squadron VA-25, called the "Fist of the Fleet," and was using the call sign Canasta. It was late afternoon, with the sun receding fast. The Skyraiders of Canasta flight made their run-in beneath a flat ceiling of cloud at 11,000 feet, typical of the "crud" over North Vietnam that always seemed to hamper navigation.

Typical for an SAR mission, Greathouse's airplanes carried four pods with seventy-six

Lightning flash —Part of the fuselage of an A-1H Skyraider flown by the "Thunderbolts" of VA-176. The stylized flash of lightning painted on their aircraft helped make them one of the better-known squadrons flying the A-1H Skyraider.

The Tonkin Gulf Yacht Club

IN SIGHT:
A fully-armed Skyraider seen through the gunsight as it flies above the karst limestone ridges near the Laotian border. It was giving a gunsight view like this to the enemy that Greathouse's flight desperately tried to avoid as they took on two MiGs in the unlikeliest dogfight of the war in June 1965.

Sting in the tail —The distinctive "Bumblebee" insignia of squadron VA-176, painted on the tail of this A-1H, must have seemed like mockery to the North Vietnamese, who lost a MiG-17 jet in a dogfight to one of the squadron's petrol-engine Skyraiders.

2.75-inch rockets (19 per pod) plus a full load of 20mm ammo. In addition, each Skyraider carried the 200-gallon (1136 liter) centerline drop tank that was de rigeur for missions up north. A peculiar feature of the Skyraider was that this fuel tank inhibited the operation of the number two speed brake, located in the central position below the tail, making the airplane difficult to handle in slow-speed situations, but pilots were aware of this and lived with it.

With the mission under way, Greathouse was warned by a radar plane that he was being stalked by MiGs.

Two MiG-17s went past the four Skyraiders in the distance to their right. At first, it appeared that the North Vietnamese pilots were chasing Skyraiders from another carrier, up ahead. But it was equally clear that other MiGs could be nearby. Every man in Canasta flight felt his own version of the anxiety that comes when you're in a contest with much faster jets. That anxiety shot upward as that pair of MiGs peeled to their left, rolled over, and turned to approach Greathouse's four Skyraiders.

Controlled by GCI (ground control intercept) operators who were watching Canasta flight on radar, the MiG-17s were being vectored to a firing pass on Greathouse's Skyraiders.

Daylight was rapidly deteriorating. The Skyraiders were snug against their ceiling of cloud. One of the MiGs was breaking away for reasons unknown, but the other MiG-17 was coming right at them. Greathouse called for jinking maneuvers and ordered his pilots to drop their centerline fuel tanks. They were coming under attack.

One of the unlikeliest dogfights of the war ensued. The Skyraiders dived to ground level in a valley with sharp outcrops of karst limestone all around. With MiGs and Skyraiders jockeying for position, one of the MiG-17s headed straight at Canasta Three and Four, Lieutenants Charlie Hartman and Clinton B. Johnson. In the number four position, Johnson, flying Skyraider number 577 and handicapped by a partial radio failure, thought that he could see the North Vietnamese pilot peering at him through his windshield. The MiG opened fire at the very instant Johnson sent his drop tank tumbling away. When the tank separated, the

Skyraider lurched violently, causing Johnson to avoid a spray of 23mm cannon fire that came from the MiG. Johnson glimpsed the spray of cannon shells, like glowing red-gold balls, and realized that they'd missed him only by feet.

Hartman and Johnson maneuvered so that their own 20mm cannons were in position to fire just as the MiG opened up.

While Greathouse and his wingman covered and searched in vain for the other MiG, Hartman and Johnson opened up with their cannons—which had never been intended for air-to-air shooting. The MiG wobbled slightly as cannon shells exploded against its fuselage. For an instant, it appeared to be on a dead collision course with Johnson. Then the MiG began to disintegrate.

The MiG-17 passed between the two Skyraiders, falling apart in midair and leaving behind a thin plume of smoke. All four members of Canasta flight saw the MiG bore into the ground and explode. There was no parachute.

Greathouse as flight leader was exuberant. Hartman and Johnson each received one-half credit for the "kill." At this point in the war only two North

POST MORTEM FOR A MIG: Still in their flight suits, their faces filled with exhaustion and elation at shooting down a MiG-17, the four A-1 Skyraider pilots report below decks. Left to right are: Charles Hartman, Ed Greathouse (flight leader), Clint Johnson, and Jim Lynne.

Vietnamese MiGs had previously been shot down, both by Navy Phantoms, so the feat of bagging a MiG with the Skyraider was nothing less than remarkable.

Air-to-air combat was hardly the intended role of the A-1 Skyraider. But 18 months later, young Tom Patton of squadron VA-176 aboard the *Intrepid* bagged another MiG-17. Although carrier-based Spads flew more than 25,000 sorties over North Vietnam, no MiG ever shot down a US Navy Skyraider.

Where the Skyraider really shone, as any number of GIs would remember fondly, was in the close air support role. Jet attack pilots who flew the A-4 Skyhawk, A-6 Intruder, and A-7 Corsair—all fine aircraft—were first to admit that the prop-driven Skyraider, despite its outdated appearance, possessed capabilities they lacked. The endurance capability of the Spad to loiter on station and its ability to carry heavy ordnance loads, delivered from a steady gunnery and dive-bombing platform, were almost too good to be true. The endurance factor and thus "on station" availability was a Skyraider asset precisely because the prop-driven aircraft burned the very gasoline the Navy was seeking to dispense with.

The survivability of the Skyraider simply had no comparison among jet airplane types: In one instance, a Skyraider lumbered back to its carrier with 230 bullet holes, some of them more than a foot in diameter. Admittedly somewhat more vulnerable to hand-held small arms because it flew lower and slower, the Skyraider simply didn't go down when hit. The Spad ended up having a superb loss record.

Landing a "taildragger" (an aircraft with a tail wheel, which stood at a nose-high angle when parked or taxiing) was never an easy proposition and landing a tailhook-equipped taildragger was more than a little difficult. The hook, of course, was designed to catch the wire on a carrier deck. When a pilot was making a good approach, a landing signal officer (LSO) signalled him to proceed with a deck landing and he duly plopped his 10 tons of Skyraider down on the ship, restrained—hopefully—by the tailhook after snagging the ship's wire. When things went wrong, they went really wrong. One A-1H veered off the deck and dangled out over the sea, the pilot looking straight down at the bow wave

The Tonkin Gulf Yacht Club

THE TOLL:
Antiaircraft artillery damage to the tailwing rudder of an A-1H that managed to limp home to *Intrepid* after a raid over North Vietnam. As the Rolling Thunder aerial campaign against the North increased, so did the enemy's air defenses. Skyraiders encountered not only guns, but surface-to-air missiles (SAMs) and an increasing number of Soviet-supplied MiG fighters.

SURVIVABILITY:
This Navy A-1 Skyraider from the carrier *Kitty Hawk* had the leading edge of its wing peeled open by Viet Cong gunfire. The Skyraider diverted to a safe landing at Da Nang, another example of its ability to survive. The Skyraider had a low loss rate and seldom went down to the first hit.

of the ship plowing through high crests (he was rescued). Another Skyraider crippled by battle damage missed the wire completely and slammed into the carrier's island. Sometimes there were fatalities. Once in a long while there was even a laugh or two, of the gallows humor variety: One pilot on *Oriskany* landed his A-1H in such a preposterous attitude, with propeller chewing into the deck and tail reaching for the sky, that deck crewmen had to chuckle even though the flier had narrowly cheated death.

On February 2, 1966, a flight of four single-seat A-1J Skyraiders from *Ranger* launched from off the coast and headed inland on a bombing mission. The Spads crossed North Vietnam and entered Laos near the Mu Gia Pass, an area of heavy enemy infiltration. Lieutenant Dieter Dengler, a pilot of the "Swordsmen" of VA-145 flying airplane number 142031, was pulling away from hitting his target when he was hit by gunfire and found himself falling end over end as flames swept over his aircraft.

Dengler blew his canopy with the emergency air bottle. As his Skyraider gyrated wildly, he unstrapped himself, threw his harness out into the slipstream, and climbed onto his seat. He was about to jump when some instinct told him to stay with the plane.

Dieter Dengler strapped himself back in and skipped over a long green mountain ridge. Peering through his windmilling propeller, he struggled with the plane and brought it down in a clearing. Dengler found himself dangling upside-down in a cockpit that was filled with heavy thick foliage, with thick dust cutting off the light. He got away from the plane and was waving at rescue helicopters when a communist Pathet Lao stuck an M-1 rifle in his face.

Skyraider pilot Dengler was held prisoner under the most barbaric conditions in Laos for six months, during which time he became violently ill and his weight dropped from 170 to 90 pounds. He was kept with American and Thai prisoners, all of whom were treated horribly. At one juncture Dengler escaped only to be captured again. Six months after his shootdown, wretchedly emaciated, clinging to life with hope and grit, Dengler with some other prisoners overpowered their captors and escaped again, deep into hostile terrain with no realistic prospect of walking out. A weakened Dengler eventually became the only escapee to reach a treeline facing a Laotian riverbank. He staggered out into the open to die. But thanks to another Skyraider pilot named Gene Deatrick things were to turn out differently and Dengler will reappear in this narrative. . . .

BY THE LATE 1960s, the Navy had to face the simple fact that it made no sense to keep more than

TAKE OFF: Crewmen secure the catapult bridles to an A-1H being prepared for launch aboard *Ticonderoga* in the Gulf of Tonkin. The bridles were attached to a catapult track. It was along this that the Skyraider hurtled as soon as the boilers below decks had built up enough steam pressure to catapult it skyward at 85 knots.

The Tonkin Gulf Yacht Club

SOUND AND FURY:
A carrier deck
officer signals
the launch of an
A-1 while a
crewman mans
the console.
Activity on an
aircraft carrier
flight deck is
frenetic but
purposeful. It is
also genuinely
dangerous.
VA-25 squadron,
called the "Fist
of the Fleet,"
lost one deck
crewman, who
was decapitated
by a Skyraider's
propeller.

one kind of fuel aboard a carrier. The A-1 Skyraider was still a very potent warplane and very much the backbone of the Navy's medium-attack force. Its intended replacement, the Grumman A-6 Intruder, had enormous potential but was also suffering developmental problems. The A-1 might well have continued on Navy ships far longer but for the fact that it was the only shipboard combat aircraft requiring Avgas aviation gasoline. The rest of the carrier force was all jet. The Skyraider's days were numbered.

Some carrier-launched Skyraider missions stuck in their pilots' minds forever. Captain Rosario

("Zip") Rausa of VA-25, the "Fist of the Fleet," went into Laos on a brooding, moonless night to work with FACs (forward air controllers) who illuminated targets with flares. This was a real test of a pilot's skill and instincts. Survival itself depended on a mastery of instrument flying and an acute sense of where wingmen were in the sky, particularly during strenuous high-G pullouts from diving runs. A brief respite, a time for reflection, came only when flying back toward the carrier.

Ten miles offshore, Rausa looked back toward the coast. His vision took in a stretch of territory from the demilitarized zone (DMZ) up to the central coast

of North Vietnam. He watched a mind-boggling display of light, glaring silver-white against pure black.

At different altitudes parachute-retarded flares were moving like slowly descending stars toward the earth. Slim fingers of ground fire jabbed up, some in solid lines, some like a sequence of hyphens. Cauliflower-shaped flashes marked for Rausa the locations where bombs were impacting.

Soon the show of pyrotechnics were over but as

Captain Rausa pressed on toward his carrier, he wondered how the terrible violence of war could produce a display of such great beauty.

On another SAR mission, trying to direct the rescue of a fellow Spad pilot, Lieutenant (j.g.) Mark Freeman of VA-152 spotted the downed airman in the center of a flooded paddy field, thrashing wildly and trying to disengage himself from his parachute. Freeman also saw several North Vietnamese soldiers running along a paddy dike less than 500 yards away. After alerting his flight leader, Freeman went low, hugged his plane's shadow, and strafed the NVA troops. In the movies, he remembered, machine gun or cannon shells always arrived one by one, stitching a pattern across the ground or water. In real life, every 20mm shell from Freeman's burst hit the waters of the paddy field at once, in a spectacular display of tiny rising geysers, bracketing the NVA troops, spinning some of them around, knocking them down.

Freeman was so low that his propeller arc, plainly visible to the pilot because of the yellow stripes painted at the prop tips, seemed likely to coincide with the only tree in the area. He pulled up and missed the tree, but not before his propeller churned up gouts of brown rice-paddy water, which splashed all over the Spad. At the same instant, NVA rifle fire thunked into his rear fuselage. Freeman hauled back the stick and went into a sudden sharp climb. He felt the world fall away from him.

While his flight leader strafed the NVA and directed a helicopter to the rescue—the downed airman was picked up and rushed back to the carrier—Freeman spotted a row of trucks rounding a bend a couple of miles from the scene. Sighting trucks in the daytime was unusual. A pilot could spend months bombing "suspected enemy positions"—the term used at the "Five O'Clock Follies," the Saigon press briefing, to describe jungle treetops—and never see such a tempting target. Though he was hit, low on fuel, disorientated, and suffering unknown damage, Freeman persuaded his flight leader that they ought to go after the trucks. They did, and produced the most remarkable secondary explosion they had ever seen—great, billowing clouds of red-orange fire punctuated by the crisscrossing patterns of enemy ammo flying off in

Minelayer—An XM-3 mine dispenser mounted on the port wing of an A-1E Skyraider. It was one of the few Vietnam-era aircraft suitable for minelaying. Only helicopters could match the Skyraider's ability to fly at slow speeds and carry similarly large quantities of mines.

The Tonkin Gulf Yacht Club

WHEELS UP: An A-1H Skyraider makes a wheels up landing on board *Intrepid* in July 1966. The nylon emergency barrier had been hauled into position after the pilot had radioed ahead that he had lost the use of his landing gear after being hit by enemy gunfire. The barrier served as a fail-safe and reassured the pilot that he would not have to make a second attempt.

all directions. It was a sight Freeman would never forget.

The Rolling Thunder campaign began with the first strikes up north on March 2, 1965, and ended with President Johnson's bombing halt on October 31, 1968; it was a period rich in new developments in carrier warfare. The Navy was assigned a significant part of the Hanoi-Haiphong region, known as Route Package VI-A, and bombed it repeatedly—although with less success in poor weather and after dark. The Alpha Strike was a new invention of the period—an attack by an entire carrier air wing, with different squadrons and different types of aircraft approaching at varying times and speeds to confuse the enemy. One Alpha Strike against POL (petro-

leum oil lubricant) storage facilities in Haiphong, consisted of no fewer than 118 aircraft from ten squadrons aboard three carriers—A-4 Skyhawks, A-6 Intruders, F-4 Phantoms, and, of course, the inevitable Spads. Because it flew lower and slower under most circumstances, the Spad really did confuse the enemy and make his task of air defense more difficult.

Innovation or none, there were more than a few naval aviators, Skyraider pilots among them, who wondered about the campaign against Hanoi. Rolling Thunder was supposed to be a "measured and limited air action" against targets South of 19 degrees north latitude and were supposed to break the will of the North Vietnamese to wage war

SPY IN THE SKY:
The EA-1F used for early warning and electronic warfare, with its large underwing ECM (electronic counter-measures) pod, was the final Skyraider to fly a Vietnam combat mission in Navy markings. In this Spad, electronics technicians occupied the rear seating space in the "Blue Room."

against the South. But the enemy's will was stronger than that and, to make the task frustrating, it was difficult to find worthwhile targets. Unlike almost all previous air wars there was no massed armies, fleets, or arms factories. There were hardly any sizable towns and these, in any event, were declared off limits to US air crews. During 1965-66, highly professional aircrews were being sent on arduous interdiction strikes against targets whose location, and even existence, were problematical. With the September 1967 strikes on POL, this changed somewhat—but not enough.

Although the idea of using the Skyraider to spray Agent Orange had been quickly rejected following Doug Francis's trial run, Navy planners kept trying to foist new missions on carrier-based Skyraider squadrons. Beginning in 1967, VA-176 on the *Intrepid* flew night missions searching for "Wiblicks," slang derived from WBLC for waterborne logistics craft. Using A-1Hs and highly trained pilots against tiny boats, many of them never proven to be involved in infiltration, produced doubtful results at best. More successful was a mission known as Midnight Express, undertaken by VA-25 in its penultimate cruise in 1967, aimed at bombing roads, viaducts, and ferry crossings—the enemy's communications infrastructure.

Critics of Rolling Thunder said that it was not always thunderous. When the long bombing campaign ended—its termination announced by President Johnson at the same time as his decision not to seek re-election—it was clear that the enemy's will had endured. North Vietnam had suffered but survived. And so would some Skyraider pilots, like Ensign Edward A. Davis ("a great resister and Yank," according to a pal) who were to spend seven years as prisoners of war in North Vietnam after being downed and captured during Rolling Thunder.

The Skyraiders of VA-25 returned to the combat zone in early 1968 aboard *Coral Sea*. On April 10, 1968, the pilots of VA-25 were the last to fly the single-seat carrier-based Skyraider on a combat mission.

But a few of the multiseat EA-1F early-warning airplanes remained. The last combat mission by a Navy Skyraider was made by a "fat" EA-1F rigged with radar and other equipment to identify threats to the fleet. It happened on September 18, 1968, and the honor went to squadron VAA-33 (formerly VAW-33), the "Night Hawks," which had their Detachment 11 embarked on the Westpac cruise of *Intrepid*. The Skyraider chapter in the Navy's war in Southeast Asia was over.

END OF THE LINE: The retirement ceremony held at Naval Air Station Lemoore, California, on April 10, 1968,to mark the A-1H Skyraider being phased out of Navy service. At this time, the EA-1F early-warning version of the Skyraider was still flying from carriers in the Gulf of Tonkin.

The making of Able Dog

BY THE TIME it went into combat in Southeast Asia, the Skyraider didn't just look old. It really was old. More than two decades had passed since a design team under Douglas's Ed Heinemann had conceived of the airplane.

The much-loved if not exactly beautiful Skyraider was known throughout the Vietnam War period as the A-1, the designation it acquired when the US system for naming airplanes was overhauled on September 18, 1962. Throughout most of its life, including its yeoman service in the Korean War, it was called the AD (signifying the attack role and the manufacturer, Douglas), a moniker that pilots transomed into "Able Dog."

At the time of its inception, however, it was neither AD nor A-1 but BT2D. This designation was based on its planned role as a torpedo bomber to replace the famous Dauntless of World War II. And the Skyraider did, in fact, launch the last torpedoes ever dropped from an aircraft in combat.

The Skyraider's origins can be traced back to a wartime competition to replace the SBD Dauntless, which had decimated Japan's carrier force at Midway. Ed Heinemann, chief engineer of the Douglas Aircraft Corporation's Navy plant at El Segundo, California, teamed up with lieutenants Leo Devlin and Gene Root to devise potential Dauntless replacements, the BTD-1 Destroyer and BT2D-1 Skypirate. Their designs reflected the intention of Navy planners to replace the "scout"

and "dive-bomber" SBD aircraft with a single-seat, single-engine, very powerful dive-bomber also capable of carrying torpedoes but no longer burdened with the extra crewman dictated by the scout mission. (The backseat gunner/radio operator—then a cult hero, typified by Roscoe Sweeney in the *Buz Sawyer* comic strip—was about to disappear from modern warfare.)

None of these BT airplanes made the grade, however, and the contract for a Dauntless replacement went to Curtiss, which produced another scout/dive-bomber, the difficult-to-fly and

The making of Able Dog

A HARD ACT TO FOLLOW:
The Skyraider came into being when Douglas's Ed Heinemann led a design team to win a Navy competition to develop a replacement for this airplane—the SBD Dauntless. The torpedo bomber was famous for its role in overwhelming Japan's carrier force at Midway in World War II.

little-appreciated SB2C Helldiver. The Helldiver was commonly known to its crews as the "beast," not because of its warlike qualities but because it was a pain to fly.

None of the early Heinemann BT designs rated a production contract, but they did result in El Segundo's personnel acquiring invaluable experience with big, prop-driven warplanes.

Ed Heinemann had based his ideas for a new carrier-based Navy strike aircraft on the Pratt & Whitney R-2800 engine only to be told that the Navy planners preferred the bigger R-3350 Wright

The shape of things that didn't come. This heavily armed SB2D-1 Destroyer was one of Douglas's early efforts to produce a new carrier aircraft to replace the Dauntless. Seen over California in 1943, the SB2D-1 failed to make the grade but it contributed to the work that eventually produced the Skyraider.

Cyclone, although it seemed to many to be too big, too powerful, for a single-engine warplane.

Dealing face-to-face with Navy people at Washington's old W-Building ten days after the Normandy invasion on June 16, 1944, and about to be defeated by a looming deadline, Heinemann stashed his design team back in their temporary lodging at the Statler Hotel and instructed everybody to roll up their shirtsleeves. Working deep into the night hours with piles of notepaper and a crude drawing board, Devlin, Root, and Heinemann created a wholly new aircraft design. What we now know as the Skyraider came into existence in that hotel room between 7 PM and 4 AM. The Douglas design team then sneaked a couple of hours of sleep, showed up for conversations with the Navy in the morning, and sold their new aircraft. At the time, it was called the XBT2D Dauntless II. The first version would be the BT2D-1.

Despite the last-minute timing, Heinemann persuaded the Navy to go ahead with his new aircraft. The manufacturer was given a difficult set of specifications to meet, however. The new aircraft had to move from drawing board to the flight test stage in nine months. A variety of weight and structural requirements were imposed by the Navy, some of which seemed exceedingly difficult to meet.

The big R-3350 was considered a very difficult power plant to put into a single-engine aircraft, and the situation loooked doubtful even after Heinemann's engineering team was joined by Dr. Milton Clausen, who was responsible for mating engine to airframe.

On March 18, 1945, a full day behind schedule, the belch and roar of a smoky R-3350 cut into the Sunday quiet at Mines Field, the old aerodrome that is today's L.A. International. Test pilot LaVerne Brown took the shiny, silvery BT2D-1 Dauntless II up for its maiden flight and soared lazily over presmog Los Angeles.

Brown put the new aircraft through a few basic maneuvers and made an easy, comfortable landing. A Douglas employee, thinking of the company's Skytrain and Skymaster transports, and remembering the firm's tradition of christening planes with the "Sky-"prefix, wondered if Dauntless II was the right name for the new ship.

It was not an easy airplane to fly that day and it was not an easy airplane to fly 30 years later on April 30, 1975, when the final mission was logged over Vietnam. Test pilot Brown cranked the new craft like a small fighter through the clear, dazzling southern California sky, found it difficult to handle, and relished every sweet moment of it. Its plain

PROTOTYPE II:
This is what the Skyraider might have looked like if this interim Douglas airplane has been ordered by the Navy. The performance characteristics of the BTD-1 Destroyer II, seen here over the Navy's test center at Patuxent River, Maryland, on September 4, 1944, provided valuable data for the team designing the Skyraider.

The making of Able Dog

TAILSPIN TOMMY AND THE DAUNTLESS: The first Skyraider was known as the BT2D-1 Dauntless II. When the plane was first wheeled out, onlookers were amazed that the upper arc of the new airplane's giant propeller was more than 16 feet off the ground. The test pilot in the hard hat is LaVerne Brown, who was best-known for his film stunts portraying the thirties comic-strip character Tailspin Tommy.

aluminum finish glinting in the sun, the BT2D-1 demonstrated performance not too different from that experienced by Brown in Corsair and Hellcat fighters.

Destined to be the last warplane in the Navy with a tail wheel, the BT2D-1 was a sturdy, simple machine, a "taildragger" with low wing, open air-cooled engine cowling, and sliding bubble canopy. The squarish wing folded at midpoint for carrier stowage. The main landing wheels retracted straight backward on sturdy oleo struts to lay beneath the lower wing with the wheels recessed

behind the main spar. The rudder on the large tailplane—an essential feature for new pilots to master—was hydraulically powered. The aircraft looked big and was big, but developmental tests and early carrier operations proved that it flew very much like the smaller fighters then serving with the fleet.

Included among the first 25 airframes built were versions for photoreconnaissance (BT2D-1P), night operations (BT2D-1N), anti-submarine work (BT2D-1Q), and electronic countermeasures (BT2D-1W), as well as a second version of the basic

design with minor changes (BT2D-2). All of this alphabet soup, as well as the Dauntless II moniker, proved too unwieldy and eventually the Navy decided to give a simpler name to its new aircraft. The BT2D-1 Dauntless II was renamed the AD-1 Skyraider.

The Navy eventually acquired 242 airplanes of the first version, the AD-1, with the now-familiar 2,500-horsepower R-3350-24W engine, as well as 35 airplanes designated AD-1Q and used for electronic countermeasures (ECM) with a jamming pod on the left wing and an ECM operator colocated with the pilot. Carrier qualifications for the Skyraider were conducted aboard the jeep carrier *Sicily* in the spring of 1946 and a few months later squadron VA-19A at Alameda, California, was the first to become operational with the new airplane.

In 1946 the huge Skyraider was not merely the biggest single-seat aircraft in the world but the most powerful. Jets were coming along, but no one knew yet whether they would replace propeller aircraft. Skyraider pilots were then the hottest rocks in the fleet, expected to have style and derring-do, charming with the ladies and brutal with their airplanes. One of them set forth to fly under the Golden Gate Bridge. In later years, more than one Skyraider pilot went aloft with his wings folded— usually by accident but once, reportedly, on a bet.

The second principal version of the Skyraider, the AD-2, was delivered to the fleet with strengthened wings, greater fuel capacity, and the R-3350-26W engine with its horsepower increased to 2,700. One hundred fifty-six were built. Some were later converted to AD-2D, to function as drone controllers. Twenty-two more Skyraiders were delivered as AD-2Q electronic countermeasures airplanes. In the AD-2 airplanes, cockpit controls were fashioned to resemble the systems they actuated, with the dive brake control, for example, looking like a miniature dive brake instead of a knob.

In the late 1940s, came the third version of the Skyraider, the AD-3, with lengthened and strengthened landing gear. One hundred twenty-four were built. AD-3E aircraft were used for early warning, AD-3N for night atack (these adding 15 airplanes to the production run), AD-3Q for ECM (24 airplanes), AD-3S for antisubmarine work as a "hunter/killer" partner to the AD-3E, and AD-3W for airborne early warning surveillance (a further 31 airplanes). The AD-3W carried two radar operators inside the spacious fuselage below and

STRAIGHT FROM THE DRAWING BOARD: The XBT2D-1 was the name Douglas gave to the concept that they sold to the Navy planners. In homage to the plane it was designed to replace, this early version has "DAUNTLESS II" painted on the tail. The folding wings appealed to the Navy as it made the plane easier to store and maneuver on carrier decks.

behind the pilot, and had APS-29 surveillance radar mounted in a "guppy" radar pod under the fuselage. This version also had a distinctive triple tail. A target-tow AD-3U airplane was also used by the Navy.

The fourth version of the Skyraider was the AD-4 (known as A-1D after September 18, 1962; the designations A-1A, A-1B and A-1C were never assigned). The AD-4 was designed for a much greater gross weight, 24,000 pounds instead of 18,500 pounds. Three hundred forty-four were built. In this series came the AD-4B intended to use "toss bombing" techniques to deliver a "special" (nuclear) weapon and armed with four rather than two 20mm cannons (194 airplanes). Also came the AD-4L, which was "winterized" for Arctic operations, the AD-4N night attack aircraft equipped with ASP-19A radar, the AD-4NA stripped night attack version, the AD-4Q for ECM work (39 more airplanes), and the AD-4W early warning version, again carrying a "guppy" radar pod (168 airplanes). In 1965, ten AD-4NA airplanes (then redesignated A-1D) were given to Cambodia, followed by five more later. These flew early combat missions against Viet Cong operating inside Cambodia.

THE FIFTH MAJOR version of the Skyraider, and the first to see widespread service in Vietnam, was the AD-5 (known after September 8, 1962, as the A-1E). This was a "wide body" or "fat face," to use

EARLY SPAD:
A BT2D-1 in 1946, carrying two 11-inch Tiny Tim and twelve 5-inch HVAR (high velocity aircraft rockets). Both the aircraft and the armaments were still in use during the Vietnam conflict 20 years later.

the term popular at a later time with Air Force pilots
at Nakhon Phanom—a variation on the basic design
with side-by-side seating in the front cockpit and
space for two or more additional crew members in
the back, beneath the azure Plexiglas canopy known
as the Blue Room.

The AD-5 (A-1E) introduced a taller fin, had the
two side dive brakes removed, leaving just the
ventral dive brake, and had a maximum weight of
25,000 pounds. Two hundred twelve were built. An
electronic warfare version was the AD-5Q (EA-1F)
of which 54 were converted, while another 239
airplanes were completed as the night attack
version, the AD-5N (A-1G). The AD-5U (UA-1E) was
a converted target tow while the AD-5W (EA-1E)
was a radar-equipped early warning aircraft. These
many versions all retained their specialized missions
in the Navy. When the Air Force and VNAF began
operating them, specialized equipment was removed
so that there was little difference between, for
example, an A-1E and an A-1G. Air Force and
VNAF pilots tended to use the term A-1E to refer
to all Skyraiders in which the side-by-side
arrangement up front replaced a single seat.

The Navy returned to the single-seat Skyraider
configuration with the sixth principal version, the
AD-6 (known as the A-1H after September 18, 1962),
which introduced new bombing avionics. Seven
hundred thirteen were built. The seventh version,
the AD-7 (later A-1J) had a more powerful
3,050-horsepower R-3350-26WB engine. Seventy-two
were built. Air Force, VNAF, and Navy pilots tended
to use the term A-1H to refer to all single-seat
Skyraiders of the Vietnam era since outwardly the
A-1J was almost indistinguishable.

A total of 3,180 Skyraiders were built. This created
tens of thousands of jobs and, during an era when
it had little else to sell, Douglas's El Segundo plant
was kept alive.

IN THE LATE 1940s when "bomber generals" and
"carrier admirals" indulged in a shameless inter-
service rivalry for budget dollars, the Navy set out
to make a point to the Air Force. The "Warhorses"
of attack squadron VA-55 were sent up in their
lumbering Skyraiders to intercept Strategic Air
Command's monster B-36 bombers inbound from

Hawaii as they approached California at 32,000 to 34,000 feet. Their faces chafing from tight-fitting oxygen masks, Commander N.D. Hodson's Skyraider pilots coaxed and nursed their protesting R- 3350 engines, forced their Skyraiders to heights they had never been meant to attain, and photographed the bombers. The pictures were to permit Navy spokesmen to tell Congress, disingenuously, that even a prop-driven attack plan could outperform the B-36.

This was hardly good preparation for air-to-ground combat missions in a shooting war, but VA-55 was ready for the real thing when the North Korean invasion of June 25, 1950, touched off a new war. Operating from *Valley Forge*, Hodson and his pilots in their deep-blue Skyraiders flew their first combat strike on July 3, 1950, against Pyongyang East airfield.

As gunfire from the ground sought them out, Hodson and his fliers rolled in to send 100-pound and

SELLING IT TO THE MARINES: Three AD-4Ws of VMC-2 carrying ECM equipment in 1955. The Marines first flew the Skyraider in combat during the Korean War where it proved its effectiveness in the ground support role.

INSIDE THE SKYRAIDER

1 Aeroproducts 4-bladed variable pitch propeller with 13-foot, 6-inch diameter.
2 Cowling nose ring
3 Wright R-3350-26WA 18-cylinder, two-row radial engine
4 Detachable cowling panels
5 Starboard mainwheel
6 Three hundred-gallon centerline auxiliary fuel tank
7 Oil tank with 38.5-gallon capacity
8 Armored front bulkhead
9 Cockpit floor level
10 Instrument panel shroud
11 Armored glass windscreen
12 Ammunition tank, 200 rounds
13 Gun camera
14 BLU-11B 500-pound napalm tanks
15 20mm cannon
16 Starboard wing, folded position
17 Armored headrest
18 VHF aerial
19 HF aerial
20 Static head
21 Static dischargers
22 Deck arresting hook, down position
23 Tailwheel
24 Airbrake housing
25 Port lateral airbrake in open position
26 Ventral airbrake in open position
27 Five-inch HVAR air-to-ground rocket
28 Rocket pack with nineteen 2.75-inch folding fin rockets
29 Three hundred-gallon auxiliary fuel tank
30 SUU-11A rocket launcher
31 Folding fin rocket for SUU-11A launcher

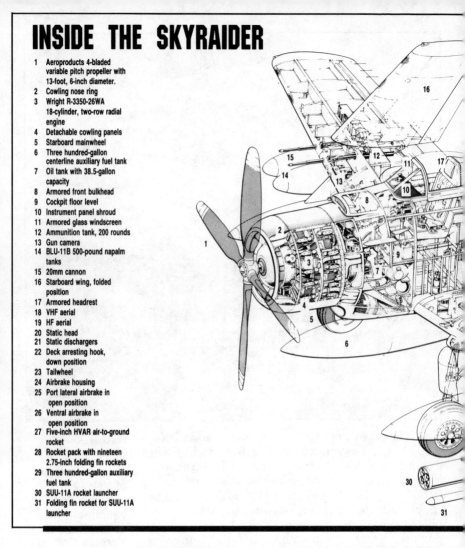

500-pound bombs splattering across the airfield's buildings, fuel dump, and flight line. Next day, VA-55's "Warhorses" bombed a North Korean bridge and began a highly successful campaign against the enemy's rail lines.

On the carrier decks the Skyraider proved to be a rugged, sturdy warplane capable of surviving Korea's tortuous extremes of seasons, searing hot in summer, near-Arctic in winter. *Valley Forge,* joined by *Philippine Sea* and *Leyte,* went into the bitter Korean winter of 1950 launching daily Skyraider strikes against convoys, and marshalling

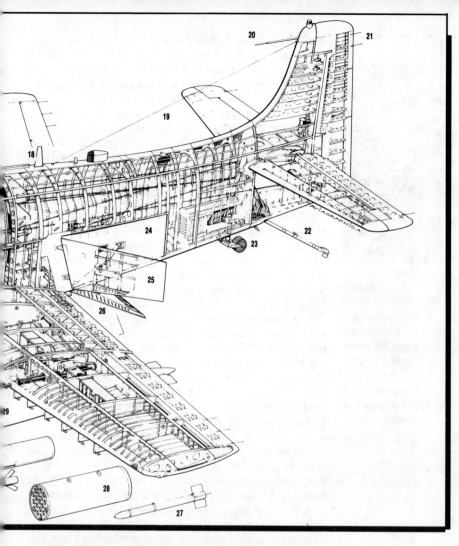

yards, bridges, and tunnels. When the Chinese entered the conflict in November and sent half a million men swarming down on the Marines at the Chosin Reservoir, the Skyraider proved its mettle flying close air support missions under the most gruelling winter conditions.

While the typical Skyraider outfit was an attack squadron (VA), during the 1950-53 Korean fracas some Spads were operated by fighter squadrons (VF) in an unusual move that gave the fighter jocks an exceedingly powerful and heavily armed warplane. The Marines operated Skyraiders in Korea as well,

Hooks away —US Navy Skyraiders with their tailhooks extended prepare to peel off one by one from the formation to land aboard a carrier deck.

including the AD-4Q, which carried an extra crewman out back behind a canoe-shaped canopy and used an array of black boxes for electronic snooping. Several times, Skyraiders were "bounced" by MiG-15s. The MiG pilots learned at their peril that nothing could outmaneuver a well-flown Skyraider and that if they got into a turning contest it meant death—especially after the switch from two to four 20mm cannons introduced with the AD-4B model. No Able Dog pilot ever got credit for a MiG kill in Korea but many a MiG pilot went scurrying back across the Yalu in shock and fright.

Although the AD Skyraider was effective in Korea, pilots became concerned that they were vulnerable to ground fire, especially in the broad underfuselage. A young pilot, Lieutenant Commander Hank Suerstedt, bucked the system by diverting eight rail boxcars of aluminum to the Douglas plant to be used for armor plating. Live-firing tests were carried out with Skyraider bellies reinforced with the precious metal. Suerstedt convinced the Navy and by 1952 Skyraiders throughout the fleet were being fitted with 5-inch aluminum plating and additional exterior steel. Losses to gunfire went down dramatically after the first newly armored Able Dogs were introduced in Korea. Suerstedt went on to become an admiral and a key decision maker in Navy attack aviation.

The Skyraider grew more and more effective in the close support role as GIs and Marines learned that they could call in ordnance within 300 feet of friendly troops. Skyraiders hugged the ground so closely that one pilot killed a North Korean infantryman with his propeller blades. Communication was not always effective, but the staying power and good visibility from the Able Dog's cockpit made bombing and strafing very accurate at pinpoint distances and no incident of friendly casualties was ever reported. It was said that the Skyraider could carry everything but the kitchen sink but Lieutenant (j.g.) Carl B. Austin proved otherwise when he sent a North Korean target a box-finned 2,000-pound bomb with a kitchen sink strapped to it.

VA-195 was one of the Skyraider squadrons aboard *Princeton* that took on the Hwachon Dam. The mighty North Korean dam had defied efforts of

UN ground troops and B-29 bombers to put it out of commission. The dam was 240 feet thick at its base with both faces fortified by rocks. An immovable object in the path of an irresistable force, it refused to go down even when Skyraiders attacked it with 2,000-pound bombs and 11.5-inch Tiny Tim rockets. The top brass decided that the only way to get the dam was to destroy the floodgates stretching between its east and west abutments—using torpedoes.

In addition to VA-195 equipped with the standard AD-4, *Princeton*'s carrier air group included composite squadron VC-35, which was using the radar-equipped AD-4N Skyraider on nightime raids. A roll call of the carrier's two squadrons revealed only two pilots who had ever dropped a torpedo before. Despite the Navy's original BT design requirement for torpedo-carrying capability, no one had foreseen that "tin fish" would actually be needed. *Princeton* had taken aboard a dozen Mark 13 torpedoes before her combat cruise. At first, nobody could remember where they were. And the carrier's ordnancemen had almost no experience with the weapons. Ensign Robert E. Bennett, one of the pilots chosen for the mission, had never even seen an aerial torpedo before.

Undaunted, on May 1, 1951, eight Skyraiders launched from *Princeton* escorted by F4U Corsair fighters. Leading the strike was the CAG (carrier air group commander), Commander Richard Merrick, described in *The Hook,* the journal of the Tailhook Association, as "a colorful aviator in the habit of carrying a K-20 camera in his AD-4Q plus a pair of 7x50 binoculars and a Luger pistol 'with a barrel as long as his forearm,' according to Bennett. During the dam strike, (Merrick) operated everything but the Luger continuously, all the while puffing on his trusty pipe."

Arriving above the river, the Skyraiders broke into two-plane sections, dodged antiaircraft fire, and maneuvered around 4,000-foot peaks to approach the reservoir. Boning up on the subject, Merrick and the others had learned that the torpedoes had a very narrow tolerance for error. Dropped too high, they would plunge into the water and sink. Too low and they would skip off the water. The Skyraider had to be at exactly the right speed, a relatively slow 160

Tin fish delivery —An Mk 44 antisubmarine torpedo is dropped by a Skyraider during a defense demonstration in 1958. From the first the Navy intended the Skyraider to have a torpedo-carrying capability. In the Korean War it earned its place in the history books as the aircraft that made the last air-launched torpedo attack in combat.

The making of Able Dog

THE GUPPY: The "fat face" AD-5 version introduced side-by-side seating up front and came in several models for different missions. This AD-5W Skyraider landing on a carrier in the South China Sea in May 1960 has a "guppy" radar installation under the belly to provide early warning to the fleet.

mph, or it wouldn't work. Six of the eight Mark 13s struck on or near the floodgates. One floodgate was blown away. The dam was breached and holed on both sides. The damage exceeded expectations. History's final use of aerial torpedoes had been a success.

In Korea, squadron VC-11 operated the AD-4W Skyraider, the early warning aircraft with radar buried in a "pregnant guppy" fairing under the fuselage. The later AD-5W Skyraider (later known as EA-1E) performed the same role in Vietnam.

One hundred thirteen Skyraiders, mostly AD-4NA night-attack aircraft, were delivered to the *escadres de chasse* of the French air force in 1960 and were

committed to the long Algerian war, where the Skyraider fought well under arduous desert conditions. Fifteen of these planes eventually appeared in Chad, used against antigovernment insurgents. The French Skyraiders ultimately ended up in several former French colonies including Madagascar, the Central African Republic, Gabon, and Djibouti.

It is from this group of Skyraiders that the civilian aviation community in the US received its "warbirds"—restored Skyraiders, listed on the civil registry with private owners but still painted in military markings—and displayed at air shows around the country, made up to look like real weapons of war.

Loitering with intent

The perfect search-and-rescue aircraft

Squadron pilot, tactical fighter, A-1E aircraft. Performs interdiction, close air support, air and surface escorts, armed reconnaissance and search and rescue missions. Maintains high qualification in air to surface delivery of bombs, incendiary, rockets and 20-mm cannon ordnance. Aids in development of new tactics and ordnance delivery methods. Maintains capability to train, advise and assist the Republic of Vietnam Air Force personnel in operation and employment of A-1E aircraft. Consistently performs duties under fire. Additional duty: administrative officer.
—Part II. "Duties," USAF Form 77, Company Grade Officer Effectiveness Report.

THROUGHOUT THE SOUTHEAST Asia conflict it was accepted that when a pilot was shot down, every effort would be made, every risk taken, to rescue him. In the early days helicopters were too few and too short-legged, communications were faulty, and the dismal weather was always an obstacle. In later years the North Vietnamese became adept at suckering rescue aircraft into flak traps, often using a captured pilot's survival radio, known as a beeper even though it had voice capability. One chopper crew settled down on a grassy field to pick up a survivor wearing US flight coveralls only to discover that he was a North Vietnamese impostor and the field was ringed with 12.7mm guns. Rescuing a man in enemy territory was a costly proposition and a rescue force often included KC-135 tankers, a C-130 command ship, fighters, electronic jamming aircraft, and of course the choppers. In one rescue attempt the rescue forces

suffered four helicopters and airplanes shot down, five men killed, and one of their number captured in addition to the survivor they were trying to save. It was an expensive proposition, but it had to be done.

It was evident that somebody needed to escort the helicopters. Choppers were an open invitation to Triple-A (antiaircraft artillery) and small-arms fire because of their slow speed and the mechanical complexity of the gearing in the exposed motor system. In the early 1961-64 period, T-28s and A-1 Skyraiders flown by Air Force Air Commandos were

Loitering
with intent

FULL FORCE:
An Aerospace
Rescue and
Recovery
Service HC-130P
refuels an
HH-3E Jolly
Green Giant
helicopter while
two A-1 Sandys,
the call sign for
Skyraiders
committed to
the rescue
service, escort
the rescue
helicopters. A
rescue force
trying to extract
a US serviceman
from the North
also included
electronic
jamming aircraft
and fighters to
silence enemy
guns. When a
man's life was
at stake in
enemy territory,
there was
almost no limit
to the resources
that would be
committed to
his rescue.

informally assigned to accompany and protect US government-funded Air America Hueys covertly operating in Laos and Air Force HH-43B/F Pedro choppers in South Vietnam. The Skyraider, which needed minimal throttling-back to escort choppers and could orbit over a rescue scene almost indefinitely, was ideal for what became known as the Sandy (rescue escort) job. No other warplane could remain overhead carrying the wide variety of cannon shells, rockets, napalm, and cluster bombs (and, on rare occasions, riot agents) to deter enemy troops from seizing a downed airman on the run. Air

Triple-A —A captured piece of enemy antiaircraft artillery (AAA) capable of firing 37mm rounds. Mounted on a four-wheel chassis, this 1938-model Degtyereva Shpagina 46-inch gun could be moved at short notice. North Vietnam's air defenses escalated as a direct response to the increased number of US missions flown against the North. All its supplies of AAA guns and SAM (surface-to-air) missiles were provided by the Soviets and China.

Force people saw the Skyraider as ideal for this role. But first carrier-based Navy Skyraiders had to show the way before a formal Air Force mission was set up when the 602nd Fighter Squadron (Commando) shifted its A-1Es from Bien Hoa to Udorn in July 1965.

The pilot of an F-100D Super Sabre or "Hun," call sign Ball 3, became the object of the first major rescue operation of the war on November 18-19, 1964. While escorting a reconnaissance flight over Laos, the Hun pilot was hit by a Laotian communist Pathet Lao Triple-A gun position, and bailed out. American aircraft led by an HU-16 Albatross amphibian headed toward the scene while two HH-43 choppers at Nakhon Phanom were put on strip alert. The Albatross pilot became the on-scene commander (OCS) and requested that Navy A-1E Skyraiders proceed to the Ben Senphan area to suppress enemy opposition.

Arriving over the thick forest canopy where the pilot was down, the Spads came under fire from Pathet Lao guns near the spot where the Hun pilot was thought to be—the highly effective hand-held beeper radio was not yet in use. The Skyraiders attacked the AAA guns, took some hits, and located a fire they thought came from the crashed Super Sabre. Across the border in Thailand, the HH-43s were launched.

The Skyraider flight leader picked up the HH-43s near Thakhek and guided them to the crash site. Flying at low level over the scene with tracers and small-caliber shells flinging around them, the Skyraider and chopper pilots surveyed the fire but detected no sign of the Hun or its pilot. In rage and frustration, they concluded that the fire was of natural origin and that they'd been risking their lives to mount a rescue in the wrong location. By nightfall, no fewer than 31 friendly aircraft were in the region where the Skyraiders lingered, but the downed airman could not be found.

With the dawn, another Albatross and a new rescue force proceeded to the area. At mid-morning, the OCS spotted the downed airman's parachute and the wreckage of his jet only 50 meters from a Pathet Lao gun emplacement. Struggling against poor weather and increasing ground fire, rescue pilots were finally able to bring in an Air America

chopper. When the chopper's copilot was lowered on a sling, he discovered that the downed flier had died of injuries from his landing. Two lessons had been learned. Better helicopters were needed—and the A-1 Skyraider was effective at covering a rescue effort.

Beginning in early 1965, the Navy posted six A-1Es at Udorn for rescue duty. Soon after, the Air Force's 602nd at Udorn took over the mission. Eventually, the other half of the Sandy team, the HH-43 chopper, gave way to the HH-3E Jolly Green Giant and the HH-53 Super Jolly Green which had the fuel and armament for long-range rescue work. Over the years, equipment and tactics were improved but the ingredients of an air rescue force remained the same from 1965 to 1972.

ON MARCH 10, 1966, flying a First Air Commando Squadron A-1E Skyraider from Pleiku, Major Bernard F. Fisher of the 1st ACS found himself leading four ships through withering Viet Cong

TRIPLE-A DAMAGE: A ballpoint pen stuck into the leading edge of the wing of a Skyraider shows a bullet hole, probably caused by a 7.62mm round from an enemy AAA position. Provided a direct hit did not strike the pilot, the controls, the fuel tanks, or the engine, Skyraiders could, and did, keep on flying.

gunfire during heavy fighting at the besieged Special Forces camp in the A Shau Valley. Major Dafford W. ("Jump") Myers who commanded the Qui Nhon-based detachment of the 602nd Fighter Squadron (FS) was flying close support right at the A Shau camp when his Spad was hit by heavy-caliber fire. Myers made a rough landing in his burning, crippled A-1E onto an airfield that by then was virtually overrun by the enemy.

A furious battle was raging at A Shau and the confusion of battle was apparent to Myers's wingman, Captain Hubert G. King, Jr. When Jump Myers went in, Hubie had followed directly behind. He had only a rear silhouette of Myers's crippled Skyraider but could see that Myers had not jettisoned his belly tank. When a huge red fireball erupted as the fuel went off, King had thought: "That's the end of Jump." But he didn't write him off. Instead he made a high-speed pass 20 feet off the battered A Shau runway. Standing his plane on its wing, he looked down and saw that the explosion had failed to consume Myers's plane. The pilot's seat was empty and the harnesses had been thrown back, evidence that Myers had leaped out and had run for cover. But where? In the dismal weather and from his poor vantage point, Hubie could not see Jump.

Hubie King never saw the enemy gunners on a ridge above Myers but one of their 2.7mm shells hit King's windshield just where the pipper of his

EN ROUTE TO BATTLE:
1st Air Commando A-1Es fly to the rescue of the Green Berets at A Shau. During the two-day battle on March 9-10, 1966, the Air Commandos logged over 100 hours over the beleaguered camp.

gunsight was located. There was a crunching sound. Had the round continued three feet farther it would have blown Hubie's head off. The windshield exploded. Glass flakes snowed around him in the cockpit.

With a broken windshield, desperately low on fuel, with a full load of napalm still on board and the wrong radio operable, King tried to call for a helicopter while also struggling to control his own damaged plane. Told a chopper was coming—he was certain nothing else could land near Myers—King had no choice but to depart and complete a risky

Loitering with intent

RETURN OF A WRITE-OFF: Outwardly, the damage does not look fatal, but Captains William Campbell and Jerry Hawkins were killed when this 34th Tactical Group A-1E Skyraider "went in" at Can Tho on March 21, 1965. Air Force records show that the Spad was "written off," but the records are in error. A year later, Major Bernie Fisher flew 132649 at A Shau and won the Medal of Honor. **INSET LEFT:** Skyraider 132649, at the Air Force Museum at Dayton, Ohio.

diversion back to the nearest airfield at Da Nang. He recovered safely after jettisoning his napalm in Da Nang Bay.

But it was not the end of Jump. Bernie Fisher, a soft-spoken man with deep convictions and an exceedingly modest manner, circled overhead and directed other aircraft in the effort to "cap" (cover) the downed Myers. Within a few hundred feet of Myers, Special Forces Captain Tennis G. Carter was firing at attacking VC point-blank—blowing their heads off with precision shots with a scope-equipped M-16 rifle. Carter was so preoccupied with defending the camp, he never realized that a dramatic rescue was taking place.

Fisher flew directly over Myers and confirmed that he was still alive but, with the enemy closing in fast, in grave danger of being seized.

There was no time to wait for any helicopter. Fisher made the remarkable decision to land his airplane. He settled down through enemy fire, touched ground, and taxied at breakneck speed through rubble and debris toward the downed Myers. Unceremoniously, he helped Myers to leap into the A-1E head first, feet out, and took off again, still under heavy fire.

Bernie Fisher had been flying airplane 132649, a plane completely rebuilt after it had crashed at Can Tho in the Delta two years earlier, killing two pilots. A Shau was the second time 649 was involved in an incident violent enough to destroy most airplanes—and not the last. Months later, 649 was badly burned at Qui Nhon when another pilot bellied-in with the centerline fuel tank still attached. In spite of all this, 649 eventually returned to Hurlburt Field to train future Skyraider pilots and was finally put on display at the Air Force Museum in Dayton.

Medal of Honor —Maj. Bernard F. Fisher, awarded the Medal of Honor at A Shau, in the cockpit of his A-1E Skyraider.

Outgoing 1st ACS Commander Lieutenant Colonel Jake Knight put Fisher in for the Air Force Cross. Others, including Colonel Ed White at wing staff, thought he deserved more. The incoming squadron commander, Lieutenant Colonel Gene Deatrick, aware that no airman had yet received the highest American award, felt that something bigger was called for in view of Bernie's courage and, in addition, his all-American image. Deatrick got on the phone to Colonel William McGinty in Saigon to praise both qualities. "I've got this family man with five kids who doesn't drink, doesn't smoke, and the heaviest cuss word he ever uses is 'Shucks!' He has just pulled off the bravest act of the war. I want to nominate him for the Medal of Honor."

The award would have been an obvious one even if Bernie Fisher had had a whole vocabulary full of cuss words. Fisher became the first Air Force recipient of the medal in Vietnam.

In the course of the war Jump Myers's 602nd Squadron went from being a Fighter Squadron (Commando) to an Air Commando Squadron to a Special Operations Squadron. Fisher belonged to the

Loitering with intent

THE RECOMMENDATION: Fisher's squadron commander's recommendation for the Medal of Honor began with: "I've got this family man with five kids who doesn't drink, doesn't smoke, and the heaviest cuss word he ever uses is Shucks. He has just pulled off the bravest act of the war. I want to nominate him for the Medal of Honor."
Nine months later at the White House, President Lyndon B. Johnson presented the first Air Force Medal of Honor to be awarded in Vietnam to Maj. Fisher.

1st Squadron, the Hobos, which went through similar name changes. The change in the mission of the squadrons was also noteworthy. Deatrick, who headed up the 1st Squadron from February 1966 to February 1967, noted the change. "Before my time, our guys' job had been to train Vietnamese pilots. When I arrived, there were no longer any VNAF pilots in the pipeline. Instead of advising and instructing, we spent all of our time flying in combat."

On July 20, 1966, Deatrick was scheduled for a Skyraider armed reconnaissance mission in the morning. Because of a radio failure on his plane, he had to delay. Later in the morning, he was ready to go again when his wingman developed mechanical problems. Again, he delayed. Two postponements with "mechanicals" were unusual for the reliable Skyraider but without them Deatrick would not have ended up where he did later in the day.

Too late for the original mission, Deatrick decided, "Let's go anyway." By early afternoon, trying to get in one mission beneath 500-foot overcast, he was flying over a rock outcrop in a stream bed in Laos. He came up the stream at low level, made a sharp turn, and saw what looked like a fisherman waving at him with a net.

Deatrick went on. But something nagged at him. "Let's go back there," he radioed his wingman. The fisherman was *still* waving at him.

"I don't get it," Deatrick thought aloud. The man on the ground could see that his plane was fully armed. "The gomers are not dumb enough to stand in the open and wave at us when we go by."

"Colonel," said the wingman, "I think I see an SOS written on that rock."

Deatrick radioed the C-130 command post nearby to ask if any friendlies had been shot down earlier in the day. The answer was no. Deatrick then attempted to call an 0-1 spotter plane in the area but, with the 500-foot ceiling, the spotter wouldn't fly. Two more A-1s joined on his wing. The man below was still waving. After much radio contact with Saigon, Deatrick finally gained permission to bring in a Jolly Green helicopter to attempt a pick-up. The HH-3E chopper came in, lowered a penetrator, and hoisted the man up. "That guy is going to be a gomer," Deatrick thought. "Soon as they reel him into the chopper, he's going to pull out a grenade and die for Ho Chi Minh. We'll lose a chopper and my ass will go from lieutenant colonel to airman third class." On the radio, Deatrick asked, "Who is the guy?"

"Beats the hell out of us. We've got him. He looks half dead."

"Is he ours or theirs?"

"Sir, this guy claims to be a Navy lieutenant who was shot down in Laos six months ago."

"Huh?"

Deatrick's A-1E flight and the HH-3E diverted to Da Nang. But it was not until months later that Gene Deatrick learned he'd pulled off a rescue of Navy Lieutenant Dieter Dengler, the Skyraider pilot who had indeed been shot down six months earlier and who had escaped from his captors in Laos. Had Deatrick stuck to his original flying schedule that day, Dengler would never have been sighted or saved.

THE SANDYS of the 602nd Air Commando Squadron at Udorn, Thailand, flew particularly risky missions in 1967-68 trying to rescue men up North. One mission started with a chain of events that began on April 26, 1967, with the attempt to rescue the two-man F-105F Wild Weasel crew of Leo

BIG DADDY: A CH-54A Skycrane prepares to lift a damaged USAF Skyraider that will eventually be repaired and returned to service. When Lt. Col. Deatrick took command of the 1st Air Commandos he was concerned at the number of unnecessary Skyraider losses. Bombing missions had become routine and enemy AAA gunners could almost set their watches according to the time Skyraiders arrived overhead. Deatrick had his pilots vary the times of their attacks and losses decreased.

Pride in their work —A Skyraider takes off from Nakhon Phanom in Thailand. Although the airbase was closed to the outside world, the men who flew from there enjoyed advertising who they were.

Thorsness and Harold Johnson, who'd been waging a one-crew war against North Vietnam's SAM sites. Thorsness's courageous attack on SAM sites a week earlier (on a mission in which he also shot down a MiG) had made him one of the dozen airmen to earn the Medal of Honor in Vietnam. But he had to wait until March 1973 to learn about the award. For by the time A-1 Skyraiders were over his position on April 26, 1967, Thorsness was already in the hands of the North Vietnamese.

Among the dozens of aircraft and hundreds of men that eventually turned away from the attempt to pick up Thorsness was A-1E Skyraider pilot Bob Russell. His wingman at his side, Russell heard a MiG call, meaning that a friendly had spotted a MiG nearby. Standing instructions in the event of a MiG call were to "pickle off" centerline fuel tank and anything else hanging out, with the sole exception of the rocket pods. Thus, Russell jettisoned his fuel and ordered his wingman to do likewise. He assumed that the his wingman had followed the order—leading to a further mistaken assumption to come.

Already sorely taxed by the unsuccessful attempt to rescue Thorsness, and in spite of the possibility of MiGs in the area, Bob Russell and his wingman proceeded to the spot where another F-105 had been claimed by the North Vietnamese. This was just a mile or so north of the Black River. The pilot of the F-105, Joe Abbott, was in voice contact by beeper and, in spite of a deteriorating fuel situation, Bob Russell capped him and pinpointed his position, right down to knowing which tree he was in.

Russell called for a chopper. One of the choppers developed a hydraulic problem and could not proceed. The C-130 airborne command ship, Crown, decreed that the other chopper could not attempt a rescue alone (rules required the Jolly Greens to operate in pairs). His voice forlorn with apology, Russell spoke to Abbott to bid him goodnight, and pointed him in the direction of the nearest water supplies and where to take cover in the hope that a rescue could be mounted the next morning. There was no choice but to leave him.

Russell had also lost visual contact with his wingman. Suddenly, the wingman called out that he was hit and burning. Standing instructions

A Skyraider pilot
loads his flying
gear aboard an
A-1E before a
mission against
the Viet Cong in
South Vietnam.
Each pilot
carried a gun,
a gun,
a knife,
a parachute,
a phrase book,
a life preserver,
a radio,
several flares,
mirrors, and
food. A downed
pilot would use
the mirrors
when the enemy
was close, and
flares could not
be used for fear
of giving away
his position.
The glare of
reflected
sunlight on the
mirror could be
spotted by
rescuers flying
overhead.

(again) were to get the hell out. Russell told him to bail out.

Two failures, frustration, a wingman who'd been hit, and fuel running desperately low (Russell thought) for both Skyraiders. . . .It was a mess. With darkness beginning to fall and his own fuel situation absolutely critical, Bob Russell made a sharp 90-degree left turn searching for his wingman—and saw a fiery object smash into a ridge.

The abrupt splash of color was almost blinding. He was certain his wingman had been killed. In fact, Bob Russell had seen a North Vietnamese SAM explode against a hill. His wingman had put out the fire and, still carrying drop tanks, had flown safely back to recovery at Udorn. Bob Russell would not be able to, however.

There was a small dirt strip over the border in Laos where helicopters sometimes touched down during rescue missions. Running out of fuel and daylight, Russell told Crown he'd go to the airfield.

Loitering with intent

Conditions were treacherous: It was still twilight in air but dark on ground. Russell got himself oriented to the airfield location and got the C-130 command ship, Crown, to drop flares over the tiny field.

Flares were something you never got used to—a dopey kind of light, pinpoints surrounded by washed-out glare. In the tricky shadows, Bob Russell's first attempt to set down in the Skyraider was unsuccessful. Now there was more than treachery facing him. As he went around, he knew he would have only enough fuel for one more try. Only one more stab. On the radio to Crown, he implored,

"I need all the lights you can give me. Everything."

Ignoring the risk of discovery by hostile forces, the C-130 pilot released all the flares he had. It was an impressive show to the troubled Russell circling overhead—not an artificial daylight, exactly, but a display of fire and of crazy shadows. "All of a sudden, there was a whole lot of light." Russell landed in the bizarre white light and spent the night camped out under his Skyraider deep in Laos. The next day he stood on his plane and watched rescue forces heading north to search for Abbott. But Abbott was already in enemy hands and on his way to long-term lodging at the Hanoi Hilton, as the North Vietnamese POW camp was known.

AS THE WAR progressed, the Skyraider acquired a peculiar device to enable its pilot to bail out in an emergency.

While the Spad wasn't fast enough to need the ejection seat found on jets, it seemed to require something more than the pilot merely flinging himself into space. More than one pilot had attempted to bail out only to collide with the Skyraider's tall and sturdy rudder.

The solution was the Yankee Seat designed by the Stanley Aviation Company and called an "extraction system" because it used two shotgun charges and a rocket motor to literally pull the pilot out of the aircraft.

The first man to be extracted by the system was Major James E. Holler, who was leaving Pleiku for a combat mission when his aircraft developed engine trouble. A big man at 200 pounds, Holler reckoned that if the extraction system "would work on this hulk of mine, it would work for anybody."

His wingman, Captain Edwin Clark, said Holler was perilously low when he went out of the A-1E. Holler landed in rocky terrain with scattered scrub trees, breaking both ankles.

On June 12, 1967, Bob Russell at Udorn agreed to go on a routine combat check ride with Jim Rausch. The pair were rolling in on a target in the fading light of late afternoon when they took some small-arms hits. Their Spad was thoroughly riddled. Over the intercom, they discussed options. In the end, they had no choice and went out of the aircraft, being literally sucked out of it by the Yankee seats. Both men were also Century series jet pilots and had tucked their feet, as if using stirrups routinely found on jet aircraft ejection seats. The forces imposed on the Yankee Seat were the opposite of those on jets and Russell's knees were badly injured by the canopy of his A-1E. He left his parachute in a tree, scurried for cover in 4-foot ferns while being assaulted by mosquitoes, and used his beeper to direct an HH-3E Jolly Green to rescue himself and Rausch.

LIEUTENANT COLONEL Jerry Ransom, who com

On the line —A guard gets drenched while walking the line at Pleiku to discourage Viet Cong sappers from attacking the A-1 Skyraiders. Humping around in the wet with an M-16 was no picnic and the Viet Cong frequently interrupted a guard's life with mortar or rocket fire.

manded the 602nd Fighter Squadron (Commando) at Udorn from November 1966 to December 1967, worked in parallel with Gene Deatrick to introduce new tactics. Ransom discovered that often the only way to suppress enemy fire was to fly directly into the communists' gun sights. Night missions were especially scary. As Ransom later recalled: "On a typical mission, one A-1 flew high, the other low. The first dove in, dropped his bombs, and climbed out as the other came in. We flew lights-out. We had to 'see' with our radios, so there was a lot of chatter. It's a wonder we didn't collide."

The Skyraider was pressed into service for the Igloo White program, the seeding of the Ho Chi Minh Trail with sensors designed to detect the movement of North Vietnamese supplies. A-1s dropped "Spikebuoy" and "Acoubuoy" devices, which measured ground tremors and sounds of movement, pinpointing the location of supply convoys. Skyraiders also escorted choppers that inserted SOG teams (special operations groups) on hush-hush missions, sometimes inside North Vietnam. The Spad had proven ideal not merely as a guardian angel in the rescue role but as a jack-of-all-trades for special duties.

Secret war in Laos

Clandestine missions against the NVA

WHILE AMERICANS WERE glued to TV news about Vietnam, a secret war was going on in Laos, run not by generals but by the US ambassador in Vientiane, the Laotian capital. The Americans fighting in Laos were a mixture: civilians running private airlines such as Air America, Byrd & Sons, Continental Air Services; Special Forces "black cover" operators, who helped harness and guide an army of Meo (Hmong) tribespeople; and Air Force 0-1 Birddog pilots in a hush-hush outfit called the Ravens.

The Ravens lived and worked at the mountain airfield redoubt of the Meo leader, Vang Pao, at Long Thien in northern Laos. They were individualists, like the A-1 jocks. Their unmarked Birddogs spotted targets for Skyraiders and fast jets coming across from Thailand. Targeting decisions were made by a small staff in Vientiane headed by a succession of American ambassadors—Leonard Unger, William Sullivan, and McMurtrie Godley—over the period 1964-70.

The setting was remote, the terrain both beautiful and hostile: slick green jungles, looming mountain passes, and cloud-covered limestone peaks. Much of the time, their enemy was the communist Pathet Lao guerrilla force. But they also fought the increasing number of NVA who maintained a presence in Laos and ran supplies down into South Vietnam via the Laotian segment of the loose network called the Ho Chi Minh Trail. From 1964 onward, the war in Laos was also fought by regular Navy, Marine, and Air Force pilots based aboard carriers at sea or at bases in Thailand (time, geography, and intergovernment agreements

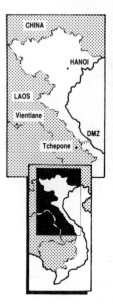

prevented them from using bases in Vietnam). Many of them scarcely noticed that they were doing battle on the far side of a borderline. Skyraider missions in Laos were routine. Yet in 1969 when President Nixon announced that "no American has died in Laos" 200 airmen had already died there. Many were Skyraider pilots.

A significant number of the casualties came from the 602nd Fighter Squadron (Commando). The squadron had moved often. After setting up a detachment at Udorn in August 1965, the squadron moved in March 1966 from Bien Hoa to Nha Trang. By May 1966, it had moved again—to Udorn, to

Secret war in Laos

SECRET WARRIOR: Richard Drury, author of *My Secret War*, flies over Southeast Asia in "Midnight Cowboy," his A-1H Skyraider from the 1st Special Operations Squadron at Nakhon Phanom. Clandestine operations into Laos were kept secret from the American public. Many of the pilots scarcely noticed that they were doing battle on the wrong side of the borderline.

rejoin its detachment. Later in the war, the 602nd shifted again, to Nakhon Phanom, or NKP. At Udorn in 1966-68, the 602nd with its Skyraiders was the principal American combat unit committed to the struggle in Laos.

The Laotian government under Souvanna Phouma had wanted US help as long as it was not publicized, but the Laotian army was unmotivated and ineffectual. At Long Thien in upper Laos, the Meo tribespeople—native to the region but not Lao themselves—were fortunate to have the leadership of Major General Vang Pao. This sparse, plain-looking man was considered a warlord by some but

Return to base —Is he back for a mission in Vietnam—or Laos? The difference was no more than a line on a map. Frequently, pilots flew on one side of the line one day, and flew the other side the next day.

a savior by the Meo in their struggle to preserve their territory and their ethnic identity.

Vang Pao had fought the North Vietnamese for 20 years and rarely strayed from the narrow world encompassing the battlefield and his headquarters, but in July 1966 he visited Udorn to compare notes with the 602nd's Air Commandos. Afterwards he wrote to Major General Charles Bond in Saigon, "A-1E pilots have been determined and consistent in leading air attacks against North Vietnamese Army staging complexes in Laos."

Vang Pao understood only too well the strain under which Skyraider pilots were waging their war. "I realize that out of 26 A-1E fighter planes which were made available for Laos only 14 remain in action. I am very sorry that you have lost so many fine pilots and aircraft to the enemy. Their courage ...(has) made them a prime target for the enemy."

The courage was beyond dispute, but at the time the tactics seemed to need improving. Every morning at 8, the 1st Air Commando bombed Tchepone. The 602nd carried out some of its missions with similar predictability. Gene Deatrick visualized a communist antiaircraft gunner looking at his watch and shrugging, "I'll finish my tea first. The Americans won't be here for another five minutes." Deatrick varied the times of his squadron's attacks and sharply changed methods. Instead of having one pilot at a time roll in for a bomb run, enabling all of the enemy's gunners to concentrate on a single Spad, two or more A-1Es came at the enemy at once. In the A-1E, with its wide canopy and empty right seat, it was very difficult to roll in on a target from the right, so pilots had started their bomb runs by rolling left. Deatrick changed this. His BDA (bomb damage assessments) improved.

The task of providing close air support for Vang Pao's tribespeople in their fight inside Laos was added to the existing roster of Skyraider duties, such as the strikes on Tchepone, by mid-1966. For a time, two of Vang Pao's cousins flew with A-1E pilots of the 602nd, helping them to identify targets among the NVA who threatened their Long Thien base.

At Lieutenant Colonel Jimmy Ransom's direction, two Skyraider pilots from the 602nd bundled into an Air America C-123 that was still reeking of cattle

excrement and flew from Udorn across a border to the secluded, hush-hush base at Long Thien. The purpose of the trip was to return Vang Pao's visit but also to "show off" Skyraider pilots to the Meo fighters who were being supported by the A-1.

During the visit to the secret Meo redoubt deep inside Laos, Hubie King and Elmer Nelson were photographed with a captured NVA 12.7mm gun that they'd neutralized in a dive-bombing Skyraider attack only a day earlier.

As the visit progressed, there were eating, drinking, and singing. Vang Pao rendered a western-style handshake with his left hand—his right had been badly injured long ago in combat. His Meo followers showed the Americans a local Annamistic ritual, then presented the visitors with traditional Meo bracelets consisting of a row of round strings worn around the wrist. Each string, their Meo hosts told them, had a separate meaning.

This one means, if you fly, they no shoot.
This one means, if they shoot, they no hit.
This one means, if they hit, they no damage.
This one means, if they damage, they no destroy your plane.

King and Nelson wore the bracelets for the remainder of their tours, were never shot down, and cut the bracelets off only after returning stateside.

Secret war in Laos

DAWN RAIDER:
A Skyraider taxis down the runway at Nakhon Phanom in the early hours of the morning. Although the A-1 was capable of night missions, pilots loathed flying over Laos at night where high ridges, low cloud, and sudden mists made conditions hazardous.

IN LAOS, nothing was worse than operating at night. Skyraiders could and did strike NVA and Pathet Lao targets after dark, but when a rescue mission had to be flown, the other components were helpless during the nocturnal hours. On Christmas Eve 1968, an F-105 pilot ejected over Laos and used his beeper to tell a wingman that he'd been hurt. The wingman told the injured pilot to take cover for the night and that a rescue effort would be mounted at first light.

On Christmas morning, a rescue force scoured the area. A pilot spotted the survivor's parachute and the A-1 Skyraiders began trolling for fire. In a trick to lure the rescue force into its sights, the Pathet

Lao refrained from firing at the Skyraiders as they
passed overhead. When no rounds were directed at
the Spads, an HH-53 Super Jolly Green came in and
hovered about the 'chute. Parajumper Charles D.
King descended from the chopper only to discover
that the F-105 pilot had been killed on the ground
by the Pathet Lao. King was attempting to hoist the
pilot's body into the chopper when he was hit by
enemy gunfire and was thrown back to earth.
Wounded and injured from the fall, King used his
beeper to tell the helicopter pilot to "pull up"
because enemy troops were about to overwhelm him.
King was later declared MIA (missing in action) and
has never been seen since. Had a night-rescue

capability existed, both the F-105 pilot and the parajumper might have survived.

Skyraider pilots considered themselves real warriors and were affronted when asked to FAC (serve as forward air controllers) for fast jets, which they considered to be wildly inaccurate. Sid Lake of the 602nd took on this role and flew to a concrete bridge crossing the river from North Vietnam into Laos.

The road over the bridge led into a Laotian ridgeline where NVA supplies were cached in nooks and crannies. There were also reports of American prisoners being held in the caves just inside Laos, which restricted air action. But the bridge had to go. Lake's A-1s were assigned to FAC for a flight of F-105s coming to take out the bridge.

When the F-105s arrived they were already close to bingo fuel (the point at which their remaining fuel would permit them only to return to base). The Skyraiders were carrying 5-inch HVAR (high velocity aircraft rockets), which had not been intended to mark targets. Lake, who was on the radio with the F-105s, attempted to use the HVAR as marker rockets anyway. He went in at low level and fired.

"Sorry," said the F-105 flight leader. "We saw your rockets leave the aircraft but we didn't see the impact."

Lake wondered, "Do you guys see the road?"

"No, can't see that either."

"Well, can you see the river?"

"No."

IGNITION ON: One of the Skyraider's hallmarks was the sight of smoke clouds pouring from the engine cowling as the pilot began the start up procedure. The R-3350 engine was notorious for being difficult to start.

Despite Lake's best efforts, the lead F-105 dropped his 750-pound bomb about a mile short of the bridge. Circling and drawing sporadic enemy fire, Lake issued new instructions to make the next pass more accurate. It didn't help. F-105 number two missed the bridge by 2 miles. Three and four were no closer.

The bridge seemed to mock jet pilots, defying constant attempts to destroy it. In the end, a flight of 602nd A-1E Skyraiders carrying 1,000-pound bombs blew the bridge to smithereens.

Skyraider pilots did not always reap this kind of satisfaction fighting in the never-never land of Laos, but they always faced danger and difficulty. A series of clandestine missions known as Shining Brass, later changed to Prairie Fire, consisted of air-supported ground reconnaissance teams sent deep into Laos (and, at times, North Vietnam) to pinpoint targets for air strikes and to make post-strike assessments of damage. Skyraiders had to cover the movement of these special operations teams. Staying with a team of men on the ground and being available when needed was an exceedingly difficult job that stretched the communications and navigation capabilities to the limit.

Skyraiders flew escort for Pony Express, the hush-hush detachment of CH-3E helicopters of the 20th Helo Squadron. These were transport helicopters inserting SOG teams (the Saigon command's "studies and observation group") deep into NVA-held areas of Laos, and North Vietnam. Skyraider pilots had to be available overhead when resupply deliveries were parachuted, free-dropped, or lowered by cable. The first SOG team recovery following a successful mission occurred in September 1967 and was followed by a series of short-duration infiltrations in 1968. Skyraiders were called upon to respond whenever a helicopter landing zone became "hot"—that is, began drawing enemy fire.

Other missions tested the interface between the Air Force and the CIA "airline," Air America. The airline's helicopters were directed by Skyraiders to rescue one Marine pilot who went down at the same junction in the same road twice in one week! When Streetcar 312, a carrier-based Navy pilot, was shot down in Laos near a landmark called the Bird's Head, George Harvey of the 1st Air Commando

Ready to catapult
—A pilot stands by to move his A-1 to the catapult for launch. Before it retired the Spad from carrier decks in 1968, the Navy flew Skyraiders on missions into Laos.

flew up in a Skyraider and found the survivor at the edge of a growth of trees. Harvey called in helicopters from Da Nang. Before they could arrive, an Air America H-34 showed up.

"Hey, Skyraider, need some help?"

As soon as the chopper had rescued Streetcar 312, the H-34 pilot turned and began chasing after the NVA who'd been shooting at all of them. The Skyraider pilot was forced to remind Air America that he had a rescued airman on board and shouldn't go off trying to kick butt with his sole door-mounted M-60 machine gun. "I didn't want quite that much help!" he pleaded, finally talking the helicopter into breaking off the Wild West style shootout.

TYPICAL OF THE secret war was the Truck Park operation. A very junior lieutenant, Jim Seith, was up with Skyraiders in Laos when a mission was ordered by the CIA-sponsored Air America.

An Air America chopper inserted some Meo "indigs" (indigenous tribespeople) into a "cold" area, a location where they would not come under immediate fire by the NVA. The indigs then marched for 24 hours while Seith and other Skyraider pilots landed, rested up, and took off to cover

BORDER COUNTRY:
A Skyraider from Nakhon Phanom heads north towards Laos. The jagged karst limestone ridges, piercing through the clouds, became a familiar sight to Skyraider pilots flying over the border country.

them again. The Skyraider could move through the air at nearly 400 mph if it had to, but by resting and covering it could also keep pace with friendly troops hacking through the jungle on foot—the only warplane with such a capability.

The Meo fighters crossed a river and ended their march in a jungle area where the NVA had hidden away a large number of trucks for the winter. The vehicles were heavily camouflaged and the NVA were holed up in caves around them. The Meo infiltrated the truck park and planted thermite bombs among the vehicles. While the Meo raiders went about their work with remarkable audacity, Jim Seith and his wingman provided cover, heaving rockets and bombs into the caves. Peering down he could see a shiny silver civilian Beech Baron executive aircraft orbiting the Meo and relaying instructions to the Meo and the Skyraiders. Whoever the CIA guy in the Baron was, he had style, Seith thought. And he had balls—circling over the scene in showy arrogance, potentially risking hostile fire.

The truck park went up in red-orange explosions that sprayed pieces of vehicle over half of Laos. The entire clandestine operation was pulled off with only sporadic hostile fire, thanks to the Spads' efforts in closing the caves.

The Meo hacked their way back to the cold LZ where the same Air America chopper picked them up. Seith landed safely at his base in Thailand without ever uttering his name in radio communications or identifying himself to the Meo or the spook in the Baron. Six months later, at home in the states, Seith's wife received 8x10 photos of the Meo blowing up the trucks, and a handmade Laotian purse. From whom? Why? No one ever said. But perhaps they were from Vang Pao's headquarters.

For four years, 1966-69, US airmen in Skyraiders and other aircraft made it possible for Vang Pao's people to resist the Pathet Lao and NVA. When it all came unglued, it happened fast.

Everything started to unravel in February 1970 when the NVA surrounded the Long Thien base and began pounding Vang Pao's headquarters. Quietly and with little public attention, the NVA overran Long Thien, forcing the Meo to withdraw.

Vang Pao and his supporters' last attempt to reverse the tide came with a major combat assault,

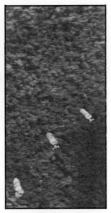

Rule of war —In Laos, as in South Vietnam, the Skyraider pilots operated with a bewildering array of restrictions, including a rule that they could only bomb along roadways. These bombs from an A-1E Skyraider are heading for a target out of view of the camera.

Secret war in Laos

TEST OF SKILL:
A Skyraider "pickles off a stick" of bombs. Bombing in the Skyraider was a test of the pilot's senses since he had no instruments to measure dive angle, mile depression, or windage. Pilots would often have to close scrutinize reconnaissance photos to discover whether they had hit the target.

beginning on January 20, 1973, when Skyraiders covered about a dozen heavy-lift helicopters inserting over 1,000 troops to reopen the Vientiane-Luang Prabang highway. The action was a military success for a time but the political winds were blowing Hanoi's way. A Laotian cease-fire of February 22, 1973, left the country dominated if not controlled by North Vietnam. A final withdrawal of the Meo did not occur until May 1975, just after the evacuation of Saigon, but by then the outcome had been ordained for several years.

Far more ambiguously than the Vietnam War,

Secret war in Laos

COURTESY OF THE CIA? These two photographs were among several received by Jim Seith's wife in an unmarked parcel six months after the truck park operation in Laos. They show Meo fighters planting thermite bombs under North Vietnamese trucks that had been stored away for the winter. Seith and his wingman provided cover for the operation.

and with less notice, the war in Laos ended. Vang Pao and his followers resettled in the US where many never adjusted. The former government in Vientiane went into a state of collapse and the NVA-backed Pathet Lao took control. There was no evacuation of Americans from Laos—a US embassy is still to be found in the capital—but resistance ended and when Americans withdrew from neighboring South Vietnam, the Ho Chi Minh Trail became, as one Spad pilot described it, "a superhighway."

Mavericks of the air

ON DECEMBER 31, 1967, the US Air Force renamed its Air Commando wings and squadrons, deciding that Special Operations was the proper term for their work. At the stroke of a pen the Air Commando was abolished as a species of American warrior. But despite the Air Force's best efforts, Skyraider people refused to shed the highly individualistic spirit of the Air Commandos, their flair for adventure, or their contempt for the "system." They disdained spit and polish. They fought the North Vietnamese with ferocity, but they also fought the top brass who had immersed them in a frustrating war with confusing rules. "A rowdy, swaggering bunch of mavericks," one officer called them.

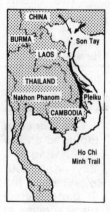

Above all, they fought the phonies. Rick Drury of the 1st Special Operations Squadron became disillusioned with a senior officer he considered incompetent and flatly refused an order to write up an award that wasn't deserved—when so many others were. In another outfit, Skyraider pilots scorned a superior who sometimes flew with them. "He flew all the milk runs. He couldn't drop bombs. It got so bad we had to take him to an uninhabited area where he could pickle off the bombs—to prevent him from hurting anybody." There were a few incompetents but they did not last very long in the high-spirited world of the Spad driver.

Though they continued to perform the Sandy mission taking on-scene command of combat rescue efforts, Skyraider pilots also performed other duties for which the new Special Operations title seemed appropriate. They were still bombing Laos, although the war there was on the decline by 1969. They were

129

Mavericks of the air

TEST BED: One of the special projects of the war was the Pave Pat II bomb, also known as the BLU-76/B, a gigantic fuel-air explosive munition that was intended to spray napalm over enemy troops. The bomb was tested in both New Mexico and Thailand but was never an operational success. Here it is seen mounted on the wing of a Skyraider about to taxi along the pierced steel plank runway at Nakhon Phanom, the closed airfield in Thailand from where three of the Special Operations Squadrons operated.

escorting SOG teams on highly classified missions in South Vietnam, Laos, Cambodia, and North Vietnam. They were working against North Vietnamese men and equipment on the Ho Chi Minh Trail.

On September 1, 1968, Lieutenant Colonel William A. Jones III, commander of the 602nd Special Operations Squadron as it was now called, launched from the outfit's new location at Nakhon Phanom, Thailand, on a combat rescue mission.

With the call sign Sandy 1, Jones was flight leader and on-scene commander of an attempt to rescue two crewmen of a downed Air Force Phantom. Jones's wingman, Sandy 2, was Captain Paul A. Meeks.

Entering North Vietnam, Jones heard Phantoms talking to the downed pilot. The second crewman had been captured. Though the survivor was in voice communication, his exact whereabouts were unclear. Jones took his Skyraiders beneath clawing

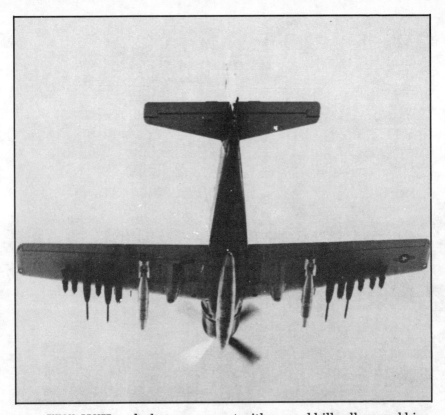

FULLY ARMED:
A Special Operations Squadron Skyraider embarks on a mission fully-armed. The thin, extended fuses are fixed to four Mk 82 500-pound bombs. Closer to the fuselage are two 1,000-pound bombs. The smaller finned missiles contain napalm.

dark gray overcast with rugged hills all around him, some with their peaks lost in the gray murk. The soup that always seemed to shroud North Vietnam on Sandy missions was now threatening Jones's flight and Jones was finding it almost impossible to get visual references to correspond to the downed airman's description of his location.

A costly misunderstanding ensued, eating up precious fuel and valuable time needed to save the downed airman. The Phantom flight marked a spot that was actually 8 miles from the downed airman. More than an hour was wasted in the wrong location before another friendly aircraft re-established contact with the survivor. Jones led Meeks toward the scene while being warned that the area was hot with concentrations of enemy 37mm guns.

Suddenly, an explosion shook Jones's single-seat A-1H Spad. Smoke churned up around him inside the cockpit. The smoke cleared. Jones heard a clattering sound. Still under fire, he flew in a zigzag pattern to make the enemy gunners' job more difficult. Ahead, antiaircraft shells exploded in his path.

The rescue of the downed airman now depended on the two items that Jones was running out of—fuel and time. Despite the damage to his Skyraider, Jones led Meeks beneath the overcast, trolling for fire to mark gun emplacements for the Phantoms. Jones went so low that one antiaircraft gun was actually firing down at him from a slope.

The gun was dangerously close to the downed airman. Jones ordered other aircraft nearby to sit tight, feeling that only he had the gun pinpointed. He brought the A-1H Skyraider around in a turn so tight that its wings were vertical to the ground. He opened up with 20mm cannon fire and sprayed the gun site with CBU-38 cluster bombs. While he was overhead, he heard the distinctive sharp sound of more bullets puncturing his plane's thin metal skin.

To make matters worse, the rocket motor in Jones's Yankee extraction seat had been ignited by the hits. Smoke churned around him and licks of flame began to work on the fabric of his flying suit. Jones levelled off and blew his canopy, certain now that he had no choice but to bail out—but when he yanked the handle for the Yankee Seat nothing happened!

Jones tried the secondary release. Nothing! Thoughts of home and family sped through his mind as air rushing into his open cockpit fanned the flames. Jones was being burned very badly while trying to radio the downed airman's position—and hearing Paul Meeks in Sandy 2 trying to tell him, "Get out! You're on fire! Bail out now!"

Bill Jones continued maneuvering in a Skyraider that, by any standard, should have disintegrated into a flaming fireball in midair. North Vietnamese gunfire continued to swirl around him. Enemy groups were pressing closer to the survivor and Jones continued to radio information about the survivor's whereabouts to others in the rescue force. Few examples of greater persistence or out-and-out bravery emerged from the entire American campaign against North Vietnam. Jones's A-1H was engulfed in a dazzling halo of flames and was trailing a thick stream of smoke that swept back into

The man on the ground —Skyraider pilots flew many missions, but they always took great satisfaction in close air support sorties where they helped out the American soldier on the ground— sometimes the ordinary grunt, sometimes Special Forces' SOG teams operating in high-risk areas.

Mavericks of the air

HO-HI

HOME FOR THE HOBOS: The 1st Special Operations Squadron's hootch at Nakhon Phanom. It was built by the pilots of the 1st SOS and was the only available recreation on the remote and dusty airfield in northern Thailand. The bar was run by a Thai called Pete, and the walls were covered with everything from aviation to pornography. INSET: The Hobos logo—artist unknown.

the confined, overcast valley, a telltale lure for enemy gunners. The aircraft was mortally damaged yet for long moments it kept flying as Jones struggled.

In excruciating pain, choking, but with a functioning radio, Jones managed to relay to Meeks in Sandy 2 and to others the location of the downed airman and the enemy gun. Then his transmitter died.

A new Sandy flight arrived to take over the rescue and Meeks peeled off to escort the crippled, burning Jones back toward Nakhon Phanom. Jones was able to make a straight-in approach and bring the Skyraider down on the NKP runway, but it was 100 percent "totalled." From an ambulance stretcher Jones gave information that led to a later, successful "save" of the survivor. Jones had become the second Skyraider pilot and one of only twelve Air Force men to earn the Medal of Honor.

IN THE EARLY years of the Hobo squadron nearly every pilot had been at least a major. In the late 1960s, the Air Force decided that the A-1 Skyraider could be safely entrusted to new, brown-bar second

PILOT'S EYE VIEW:
The cockpit of Jim Seith's Skyraider. With many versions of the Skyraider available, and just as many modifications, instrument panels varied from aircraft to aircraft. The basic layout was similar to that of many World War II aircraft.

lieutenants. Letting these clean-cut, wet-behind-the-ears kids be pulled aloft by the groaning R-3350 was an idea not fully accepted by senior officers, but most of the young guys excelled.

Among the "second johns" who joined the Skyraider operations were lieutenants Verne Saxon, Jim Seith, and Jimmy Doolittle (grandson of the aviation pioneer and Tokyo raider, and himself a first lieutenant, having completed other duties before flight school). By the time they arrived in June 1969, the Spad operation was concentrated at Nakhon Phanom, or NKP ("Naked Fanny" to an earlier generation), the bare and dusty airfield in northern Thailand that was an enclosed world of its own. Not much was said in public about what happened there. No journalists were ever permitted at NKP.

Much of the airfield itself was PSP (pierced steel planking) rather than pavement. Jim Seith found that missions were being flown into North Vietnam (although no further north than a key landmark, Bat Lake) and that the Spad typically carried napalm or 500-pound bombs, the old 250-pounders having been replaced in inventory by this juncture. Young pilots, just like older ones, loved the A-1 Skyraider with its special smell of oil and burnt cordite, its 14-foot propeller, its ability to toss bombs. One of them pointed out that the airplane never suffered rust problems, not even in the corrosive climate of Southeast Asia, because the internal oil drips protected the metal. In the late sixties, the Skyraider was still loved, still appreciated. But the lieutenants, like the majors, sometimes kicked the airplane in frustration. Its turbochargers were not so good. Instrument panels varied from one aircraft to another. Its lighting system was suspect. In June 1969, Seith saw a pilot killed at NKP because his lights failed at night. The pilots always wore flashlights dangling around their necks.

Second john —Lt. Jim Seith at Nakhon Phanom in 1969. Fresh from flying school, the new breed of young second lieutenants quickly grew used to the Skyraider and its infuriating habits.

Jim Seith quickly became accustomed to code names—slang terms, really—for the peculiar war being fought from NKP by high-spirited individualists in the veteran Skyraider. Hobos, Zorros, and Fireflies were billeted all around him. Nimrods, Nails, and Candles sometimes drank beer with him, as did an occasional Sun Dog FAC. Seith, Doolittle, Rick Drury, and others were flying combat missions into places like Steel Tiger and Barrel Roll.

Hobos, Zorros, and Fireflies were the three Skyraider squadrons—the 1st SOS, 22nd SOS, and 602nd SOS (though the last-named was usually identified by its rescue mission and called Sandy). The 1st SOS, the former 1st Air Commando, had the primary job of seeding the Ho Chi Minh Trail with sensors. The 22nd did night work, while the primary mission of the 602nd was combat rescue. Nimrods, or Nims, were the Douglas B-26 bombers operating from NKP—rebuilt since their problems earlier in the war when the B-26 was famous for having its wings fall off—and they worked closely with the A-1s on missions against the trail. Candles were C-123 cargo ships that dropped flares at night. Nails were the forward air controllers, or FACs, who belonged to the 23rd Tactical Air Support Squadron at NKP.

Steel Tiger and Barrel Roll were locations in Laos where bombing raids were flown. A Sun Dog FAC was a controller operating in another country that wasn't talked about much—Cambodia.

Seith found that he thrived on the challenge of taking the big Skyraider down into the valleys to confront danger. Of the enemy's many weapons, he most feared the ZSU-23 rapid-fire antiaircraft gun, which looked like a hose when it poured out rounds at night. Night missions often consisted of two Skyraiders, the "high guy" and "low guy," who took varying degrees of risk against those guns and who never, ever, became really accustomed to bombing by flarelight. Once dropped by a Candle, a flare was a damnably difficult thing to work with—hanging from a parachute, swaying back and forth while putting out a blinding pinpoint of light, and reflecting against valley walls. You could get fixation. Or you could get disorientated. A hoochmate of Seith's made a split-S maneuver, went down in a valley to strafe some NVA, hit a tree, and was starting to recover when a flare confused him.

Thinking he was climbing, he actually flew straight down into a valley slope. The Skyraider was one tough airplane, but they never found much when you flew it into the ground.

PERHAPS THE LEAST-KNOWN Skyraider outfit, because of its short life, was the 6th Special Operations Squadron at Pleiku, in existence only from mid-1968 to late 1969. Lieutenant Colonel Alexander E. Corey took command of the 6th after its first skipper was killed in combat on an early mission. The 6th used the call sign Spad (to add to history's litany of Hobos, Zorros, and Fireflies) and had a drinking hooch called the Spad Bar. The primary role of the 6th SOS was to cover the helicopter insertion of SOG teams in South Vietnam and Laos, as well as to handle search-and-rescue in South Vietnam, while the 602nd performed the latter role up north.

Spad commander —Lt. Col. Alexander E. Corey, commander of the 6th Special Operations Squadron at Pleiku. The 6th used the call sign Spad. Its duties included covering the insertion of Special Operations teams in South Vietnam and Laos.

Throughout the conflict, Skyraider pilots struggled to cope with what one pilot called "rules of conduct concerning aerial warfare that limited us unbelievably." They were not allowed to attack anything beyond 15 feet off any road. They had to have an FAC who had received permission from the local civilian official or from the area commander in order to drop any bombs anywhere. At various times, other restrictions were imposed. When a Sandy was shot down by a MiG, US warplanes were prohibited from attacking the bases where the MiGs were stationed. (The prohibition was eventually lifted in 1972.) Because the jet community in the Air Force scorned the faithful Spad, Skyraiders were often disguised in official communiqués as "utility aircraft" while Skyraider pilots returned from their combat tours to find themselves denied choice flying assignments. It was small wonder that they became a tight-knit clannish breed. Outcasts of a sort as far as the system was concerned, they took pride in being Hobos, Zorros, Fireflies, Spads, and Sandys.

The Sandy function was such an inbred part of the Skyraider story that pilots of the wheezing, belching A-1 aircraft almost took it for granted when they had to attempt to rescue their own. On March 18, 1969, Skyraider pilot Jim Egbert, with the Da Nang detachment of the Pleiku-based 6th SOS, was scrambled on such a mission. As Egbert recalled: "I

One of our own —The crew of a rescue helicopter pose with Capt. David Lester, an A-1E Skyraider pilot who had parachuted from his burning aircraft over North Vietnam and landed in a tree 100 feet above the ground where he stayed until rescued an hour later. A natural affinity existed between Skyraider pilots and helicopter teams thanks to the Sandy search-and-rescue role, where Skyraiders flew escort for the rescue helicopters.

"I was on alert in Da Nang and we got scrambled because an aircraft had been shot down. It happened near the brow in southern Laos, not far from Pleiku airbase.

"My flight arrived on the scene and there were already A-1s from Pleiku circling the area. We found out that the aircraft shot down was an A-1—Lieutenant Colonel Vic Cole, a very good friend of mine. He had flown lower than he should have and a 37mm antiaircraft gun had blown off his right wing.

"The airplane started to roll immediately and Vic ejected (using the Yankee extraction seat) and the only thing that saved him was that the airplane kept flying and he went out in a horizontal position. Because the bad guys were following the airplane when it crashed they didn't really see Vic's chute open.

"His chute opened very close to the trees and he swung once and he was in the clear. When Vic landed he was in some very high trees and he really got bruised up and scratched and one of his legs was really bruised, but other than that he was in good shape.

"He took out his radio immediately and was in contact with overhead aircraft and support aircraft. When I arrived on the scene there were already some A-1s on station and we proceeded to interdict the area, suppressing the guns that had shot Vic down. We found that there were more guns than we realized and so we brought in some 'fast movers,' jet aircraft F-4 types, to assist, and after about an hour we had suppressed the area enough that it was safe to bring the Jolly Green in and put him into a hover to pick Vic up.

"He had asked Vic to climb a ridgeline because there appeared to be a bare spot on top and it would be easier for the Jollies to get him. It took him a while to climb up that precipitous ridge and when he got there he walked right into a North Vietnamese camp. Luckily all the North Vietnamese were gone. We laid down a wall of smoke so that if there were guns in the area they would not be able to see the Jolly Greens hover, and we picked up Vic and brought him back to Pleiku." Cole stepped out of the helicopter at Pleiku with a very dirty face and a broad grin.

The use of Skyraiders for special missions reached

Mavericks of the air

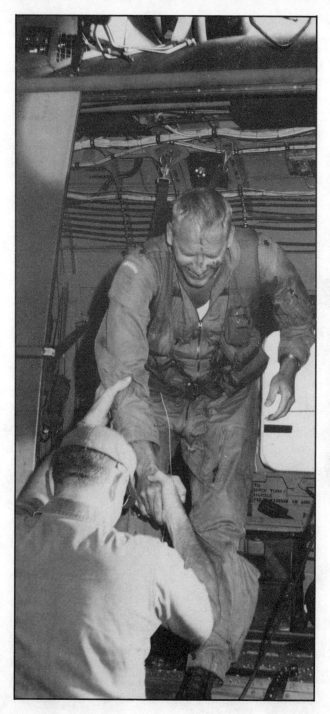

ONE OF OUR OWN:
Skyraider pilot
Vic Cole
of the
Pleiku-based
6th SOS was
shot down on
a mission inside
Laos. Other
Skyraiders
covered the
area while an
HH-3E Jolly
Green helicopter
swooped in to
pull Cole off a
ridgeline
crawling with
NVA soldiers.
Cole's injuries
were minor,
caused by
his parachute
landing in the
trees.

NAME CHANGE:
"The Naked Lady" was the name on this A-1J Skyraider when Maj. Jim Egbert arrived at Pleiku. Egbert told his crew chief he wanted it changed to"SuNanSam." The crew chief did not approve. Since no Skyraider pilot could afford to offend his crew chief, Egbert told him:"It's an obscene term in Chinese." The crew chief relented. "SuNanSam" was actually the nickname of Egbert's son and had no Chinese meaning at all.

new drama with the 1970 attempt to rescue American prisoners of war at Son Tay, North Vietnam. Two Air Force C-130s were sent from the US to act as navigation pathfinders, leading a formation of helicopters and A-1 strike aircraft to Son Tay. The rescue force took off from Thailand shortly before midnight on November 20, 1970, with six choppers behind the designated C-130.

The Son Tay raiders crossed into North Vietnam 1,000 feet above the ground, using the terrain to mask their flight path as much as possible. Rivers served as checkpoints for navigation by radar and infrared. The lead C-130 delivered the formation to the planned point three miles west of the objective, on course and within two minutes of the scheduled time. The second C-130 brought the Skyraiders in behind the helicopter force and joined the first leader overhead, dropping markers during the assault.

While Skyraiders orbited the area to keep down hostile fire, the assault force struck Son Tay in a precision raid that was perfectly executed without casualties—but, as the world now knows, no prisoners were there.

The war entered a new phase with North Vietnam's Easter invasion of March 30, 1972, and with President Nixon's decision to resume sustained bombing of North Vietnam in a campaign that became known as Linebacker.

The new level of fighting gave a new lease on life to the Sandy pilots, who now had to cover rescues in heavily defended North Vietnam on a day-and-night basis. It was a new war. But it was really a war of fast jets and smart bombs, not of prop-driven Spads and bombing via Kentucky windage. The 1972 fighting came after the American part of the Skyraider story was virtually finished, or at least in its final spasm.

Ho Chi Minh, now deceased, had said that his people would win because they were more patient and could outlast the Americans. The Skyraider was soon to be used exclusively by the VNAF under a policy of "Vietnamization" that seemed, to some at least, to prove Ho right.

HAND PAINTED:
One of the first SOS Skyraiders at Nakhon Phanom to sport a shark's teeth mural on the cowling nose ring.
The design was borrowed. It was traditional on many of the junks that sailed the waterways of Southeast Asia.
The oil drips on the centerline fuel tank were also traditional—no Skyraider was complete without them.

143

A bang and a whimper

CHAPTER

8

The Spad in the last days of South Vietnam

RICHARD NIXON took office on January 20, 1969, not least because he'd made it known that he had a plan to end the war. The turning point in US policy came in August 1969 when the president on a visit to Guam enunciated what became known as the Nixon Doctrine: Henceforth, the US would look to its Asian allies to supply the manpower needed for their defense.

The word "withdrawal" was made taboo by the White House and other terms were used to tell the world and Saigon's President Thieu what was going on.

The US would continue to provide aid, technical help, and air and naval support but no longer any ground troops. Under the Vietnamization scheme, South Vietnam would take over the ground combat role right away. Before much longer, South Vietnam would be able to defend itself.

Because the A-1 Skyraider was by far the most successful aircraft flown by South Vietnamese pilots, the Vietnamization program meant that the VNAF needed more Spads, fast. The Spad had done a magnificent job as the Sandy rescue escort, but by 1971 age, enemy action, and Vietnamization had taken such a toll that fresh supplies were needed. Douglas proposed reopening the factory line and manufacturing a turboprop version, but with the American role in the war winding down this was not the time to begin new production.

Because of the turnovers to the VNAF, the inventory of American Skyraiders in the combat zone went down dramatically, to a point where only a few airframes were left to carry out the Sandy mission and all other duties were given to other

145

A bang and a whimper

DOING IT THE HARD WAY: A-1H Skyraider number 132577 of the 2nd Special Operations Squadron was hit by 37mm gunfire that caused a hydraulic failure of the landing gear on a combat mission in December 1968. Coming in to land at Ubon in Thailand the pilot set down with no wheels, badly chewing up the underside of the aircraft. The propeller was totally destroyed—but the plane and the pilot survived.

types of aircraft. In 1969, more than 110 Skyraiders had been packed cheek-to-jowl on the flight line at Nakhon Phanom. By March 1972, the number was down to sixteen. With only these committed to the conflict and no role for the Skyraider envisaged elsewhere in the world, the US Air Force reluctantly ceased training A-1 pilots. At Hurlburt Field, Florida, one of the Skyraiders used to train new guys was mounted on a plinth and placed on outdoor display.

In 1970, as part of the effort to improve Vietnam's forces, a number of VNAF Skyraiders were retrofitted with new R-3350 engines. Just as the A-1 was never an easy aircraft to fly (the way some

planes are, as if intended to forgive pilot error by even the most hammer-handed), the otherwise sturdy and reliable R- 3350 had never been an easy power plant to maintain, repair, or use. The pun was that the Wright engine was the wrong engine and this proved true for those VNAF pilots attempting to start up an R-3350 that was either too new or too old.

The pilot had a chip detector light (red) and a fuel detector light (amber) to warn him if he had an oil pressure problem. These instruments were in different locations on different Skyraiders and sometimes did not get the attention they required. A pilot who did not pay scrupulous attention might

A bang and a whimper

GETTING GOING:
A crew chief gives the thumbs up to the pilot of "Miss Judy" as they go through the starting procedure at Nakhon Phanom in October 1972. The Skyraider was a notoriously difficult aircraft to start: it was prone to backfiring, and often required an auxiliary power supply. This photo is among the last ever taken of American-operated Skyraiders in Southeast Asia. By this time, nearly all Spads had been turned over to the VNAF.

find himself having to restart in midair. "The loudest thing you ever heard," said one, "was the engine quitting."

If it happened while taxiing on a runway you could sometimes restart with the plane's battery rather than suffer the embarrassment of having to reconnect an auxiliary power unit—but you were certain to be the butt of bad jokes at the club. If it happened in flight , the prop continued windmilling, the mags (magnetos) kept sparking, the pistons kept going up and down—and you fell like a rock, in dead silence. Usually the R-3350 quit in flight because you'd forgotten to switch tanks. Sometimes the D-handle fuel selector got stuck and you couldn't

switch tanks. All of these problems were solvable with a thorough preflight check but engine and airplane were totally unforgiving to the pilot who lapsed.

Even an ordinary engine start-up on the ground was no simple proposition if the Skyraider's power plant was too new or too old, and some VNAF pilots never got the hang of it. The pilot had to signal a crew chief to hook up the auxiliary power unit. Then he'd twirl a finger to signal that he was going to start the prop and wait for the crew chief's thumbs-up. The pilot was now ready to use starter switch and primer switch. Pushing the starter, he turned the engine through 16 blades (four turns of the four-

Repair shop —A rapid area maintenance (RAM) team mechanic gets to work on an R-3350 engine after its removal from a Skyraider. The RAM teams were composed of American civil service aircraft mechanics on assignment to USAF. After the US withdrawal maintenance was undertaken by Vietnamese mechanics.

bladed prop). Then, on getting a thumbs-up, he would turn the mag switch on, wait one second, hit the primer, and ease the throttle forward. Too quickly, and the engine would backfire—dangerous to the R-3350 and by tradition worth a case of beer to the crew chief. Too slowly and the engine would die and have to be restarted.

IN ITS COMBAT ROLE, the A-1 Skyraider met a new enemy in the North Vietnamese Easter offensive of March 30, 1972. For the first time, Hanoi's troops had large numbers of SA-7 Strella shoulder-mounted surface-to-air missiles (SAMs). Three VNAF A-1s were shot down by SA-7s in the two days at the beginning of May 1972, while the war moved into a period of heavy fighting that preceded the cease-fire and American withdrawal. VNAF Skyraider pilots learned that they had to see an SA-7 round coming and had to "jink" to avoid it. Pilots began dropping their bombs from higher altitudes than previously, with less accuracy.

The Easter invasion also brought with it North Vietnam's first use of tanks in conventional battle, and the Skyraider suddenly found itself pitted against PT-76 and T-54 tanks. During a battle at Quang Tri in April 1972, Vietnamese pilots came within perilously close distance of friendly troops as they made repeated dive-bombing runs on NVA armor, helping to destroy 13 of the enemy's 16 tanks.

In some locations, the Skyraider was the only weapon to impede the progress of North Vietnam's tanks. Some VNAF pilots flew as many as six to eight missions a day. Most types of ordnance were relatively ineffective against a tank's thick armor. The trick was to trap the crew inside the vehicle and kill them with the concussion or heat from Skyraider-launched rockets. The Easter offensive failed in every respect to bring about a victory for Hanoi on the battlefield and the role of the A-1 Skyraider had much to do with the enemy's failure.

AMERICAN SKYRAIDER pilots were now stationed only at Nakhon Phanom. The parent unit, the 56th Special Operations Wing, was under enormous pressure to make A-1 airframes available to the South Vietnamese.

The Sandy mission was turned over to the Vought

A-7D attack plane, that began to arrive in October 1972, just as Henry Kissinger proclaimed that peace was at hand. The A-7D, known to the Navy as the Corsair II although the Air Force never adopted the name, was the only jet aircraft that seemed suitable for the Sandy role. It performed well. The 3rd Tactical Fighter Squadron with A-7Ds was designated for the rescue escort mission on November 2, 1972.

A-1 Skyraiders flew their last Sandy mission on November 7. An Army UH-1 Huey chopper had gone down near Quang Ngai with seven people aboard. Flying in low murk, heavy rain, and wind as a typhoon swirled around them, the Skyraiders located the seven survivors, pinned down nearby enemy troops with 20mm fire, and directed a rescue helicopter, which snatched them to safety. This was the last mission of its kind and was also the last mission by the First Squadron, which was being inactivated. From now on, the Skyraider story was to be all Vietnamese.

United States combat operations ended on January 27, 1973, with the signing of the Paris peace accord. Now, it became necessary for South Vietnam to shoulder its own defense not merely on

SHIELDS OF WAR: The seven VNAF squadrons that flew Skyraiders always managed to maintain the smartest-looking Skyraiders, whether during the early years when they had the gray-white finish shown here or in the latter stages of the war when they were camouflaged. VNAF squadrons indulged in elaborate emblems and devices, often medieval in design.

the ground but in the air. The VNAF had received
about 310 Skyraiders but had lost about 210 in
combat and in operational incidents. With no more
Skyraiders left to give, the US began stripping its
own assets to provide new jets—Cessna A-37s,
Northrop F-5s,—and the VNAF grew faster than it
could sustain itself. Some of the arms transfers of
new aircraft were a bargaining tool, to gain
President Thieu's acquiescence to the armistice
agreement, but some were simply more than the
South Vietnamese could handle.

By December 1972, Saigon had the fourth largest
air force in the world. Manpower had reached 61,147
in 65 squadrons. Programmed and authorized to
have 1,852 aircraft, the VNAF had 2,075 (a massive
reinforcement effort known as Enhance Plus
increased the figure from 1,397 in June, although
only 28 Skyraiders were included). In its haste to
be certain that the VNAF was adequately equipped
(once the cease-fire took effect, no additional
equipment could be introduced), the US
inadvertently helped to build an air force that was
too big to be effective.

As the A-37 and F-5 jets became more common-
place, fewer South Vietnamese pilots flew the
Skyraider. Of seven squadrons that had flown the
Spad, five had now made the transition to jets.

Having depleted the US Air Force of its Skyraiders, the VNAF now put all of its Skyraiders into storage at selected airfields. Some of the A-1s had been in combat for nearly a decade and their remaining life expectancy was short. The purpose was to free up jets for combat use, at a time when Hanoi was demonstrating that it intended to continue the fight. The Skyraider was not quite out of action yet, however.

BY THE SPRING of 1975, North Vietnam was heavily on the offensive. President Thieu and US Ambassador Graham Martin assured everyone that the end was not in sight and no one listened. When Martin refused to order an evacuation, a few intrepid Foreign Service officers acted on their own to get South Vietnamese relatives, coworkers, and friends out of the country. Some VNAF pilots started paying more attention to maps and navigation checkpoints that would help them flee to Thailand or the Philippines, but many kept on fighting. For these, the war truly had no end. Some had been fighting for two decades. There was no place to rotate to, not from here.

When Ban My Theot fell, people began to think the impossible. When Da Nang fell, the impossible

THE SOLUTION:

As Viet Cong mortar and rocket attacks became more frequent, aircraft had to be protected in individual revetments to keep the effect of one lucky hit from wiping out an entire flight line. The first revetments were open-top three-sided concrete and sandbag bunkers. But the risk of sparks from a fire in one revetment spreading to another led to these reinforced hangars.

became the inevitable. Through March and April 1975, the North Vietnamese marched inexorably southward. At least four dozen A-1H Skyraiders had been taken out of storage and were among the VNAF aircraft resisting the final onslaught. But now, with the enemy equipped with SA-7 missiles, even the indefatigable A-1 Skyraider was no longer as immune to enemy action as it had once been. On April 30, 1975, vice-consul Peter Orr looked out from his office in the visa section at the American embassy to see Marines using power chain saws to cut down trees.

"What," Orr asked, "are you guys doing?"

"Sir, we're making landing zones for helicopters."

It was the last day. Orr and other remaining Americans were the final passengers in the evacuation of Saigon—Operation Frequent Wind—brought out by chopper. Many Vietnamese escaped, too, including at least a dozen Skyraider pilots (one single-seat VNAF aircraft landed in Thailand with two men in its confined cockpit). But many had no reason to escape. There was only that final fate of war—to fight to the end.

In a final moment of futility and courage, a VNAF AC-119G gunship flanked by two A-1H Skyraiders took off from Tan Son Nhut as NVA troops were coming through the wire on the airfield perimeter.

Weaving through gunfire and crisscrossing SA-7 missiles, the gunship and the two Spads made a last-ditch stand within view of much of the population of Saigon. Repeatedly, the VNAF warplanes flew into enemy fire in order to unleash their own shells and ordnance and to slow down the advance. Finally the AC-119G and one A-1H were both blown out of the air by SA-7 missiles. The remaining A-1H Skyraider—the last aircraft to fly in combat in Vietnam—was last seen heading up the Saigon River in the direction of more enemy, trailing smoke.

In a sense, the Skyraider story ended with both a bang and a whimper—the impact of the NVA takeover and the quiet disappearance of the faithful Spad from the scene. With the evacuation of Saigon, an armada of VNAF airplanes escaped and brought their pilots and passengers to Thailand, Malaysia, the Philippines, the deck of the USS *Midway*, and elsewhere. Relatively few Skyraiders got out.

After their victory, the North Vietnamese impressed dozens of VNAF warplanes into their inventory. The Skyraider was not among them. For whatever reasons, Hanoi's pilots did not—perhaps could not—fly the wheezing, grunting, oil-spewing Spad. Were the A-1 and the R-3350 more than they could handle? It would be nice to think so.

DISCHARGED:
The ultimate indignity or the final honor for a Skyraider— showing up on the US civil registry as a privately owned airplane? This Skyraider was one of the first to be privately owned in the US after being sold as surplus, and is seen at an air show in 1979.

AAA	— Antiaircraft artillery.
AK47	— Soviet 7.62 mm automatic assault rifle (Kalashnikov). Individual infantry weapon in USSR and communist countries. Effective range is 400 meters.
ACS	— Air Commando Squadron (USAF).
ARVN	— Army of the Republic of Vietnam.
ATU	— Aviation Training Unit.
BDA	— Bomb (also: battle) damage assessment.
CBU	— Cluster bomb unit.
DMZ	— Demilitarized Zone.
Dustoff	— Helicopter extraction, usually medical—also the radio call sign of medevac helicopters.
ECM	— Electronic countermeasures.
EW	— Electronic warfare.
FAC	— Forward air controller; a fighter pilot flying in a liaison aircraft or on the ground, directing air strikes against ground targets.
FFAR	— Folding fin aircraft rockets.
FS(C)	— Fighter Squadron (Commando) (USAF 602nd only).
GCI	— Ground control intercept.
Hobos	— Nickname and call sign for the 1st Special Operations Squadron.
HVAR	— High velocity aircraft rockets.
Intel	— Intelligence (service slang).
Jolly Green	— Nickname for large USAF rescue helicopters.
LZ	— Landing zone.
M-61	— Vulcan cannon.
MACV	— Military Assistance Command Vietnam.
MAG	— Marine Air Group, such as MAG-12, MAG-13.
MiG	— Soviet-built fighter aircraft flown by North Vietnamese pilots.
MiGCAP	— Combat air patrols for MiGs.
NAS	— Naval Air Station.
Napalm	— A jellied gasoline mixture used in incendiary bombs.

Glossary

NKP	— Abbreviation for Nakhon Phanom, a USAF airbase in Thailand.
NVA	— North Vietnamese Army.
POL	— Petroleum, Oil, Lubricants.
POW	— Prisoner of war.
RESCAP	— Combat air patrol for rescue operations.
Rolling Thunder	— Bombing operation against North Vietnam from 1965 to 1968.
SA-2	— Soviet-built surface-to-air missile system.
Sandy	— Call sign of the 602nd SOS engaged in search-and-rescue operations.
SAM	— Surface-to-air missile.
SAR	— Search and rescue.
Skyhawk	— Nickname for Navy/Marine Corps A-4 attack aircraft.
SOP	— Standard Operating Procedure.
Sortie	— Operational flight by a single aircraft.
SOS	— Special Operations Squadron.
SOW	— Special Operations Wing.
Spad	— Nickname for A-1 Skyraider. It was also the call sign of the 6th Special Operations Squadron.
TACAN	— Tactical air navigation system providing direction and distance information.
Taildragger	— Term for an aircraft with the two main wheels located in front of the center of gravity and a single wheel placed at the tail.
TFS	— Tactical Fighter Squadron.
Thud	— Nickname for the Republic F-105 Thunderchief.
Triple-A	— Antiaircraft artillery.
USAF	— United States Air Force.
USN	— United States Navy.
VC	— Viet Cong.
Vietnamization	— Process by which the entire US war effort was transferred to Vietnamese control.
VNAF	— (South) Vietnamese Air Force.

About the Author

Robert F. Dorr

ROBERT F. DORR is a leading aviation writer specializing in the history of the US Air Force and air warfare.

The author of sixteen books and a thousand magazine articles on the US Air Force and the Southeast Asia war, Bob Dorr is a member of the Tailhook Association and the Red River Valley Fighter Pilots Association. A pilot and parachutist, Bob Dorr has also been a participant in the US Air Force's history program.

Born in Washington, DC, in 1939, he became interested in aviation during childhood and first began badgering government archivists for aircraft photographs when he was 13 years old. He served in the US Air Force in Korea, in 1957-60, and later studied the Korean and Japanese languages at the Monterey (Calif.) Institute of Foreign Studies.

Since 1965 Bob Dorr has been a career Foreign Service officer with the Department of State and has been posted as a diplomat in Tananarive, Seoul, Fukuoka, Monrovia, Stockholm, and London. He is currently assigned to the department's Bureau of Intelligence and Research (INR) in Washington, DC. He lives in Oakton, Virginia, with his wife Young Soon and two boys, Bobbie and Jerry.

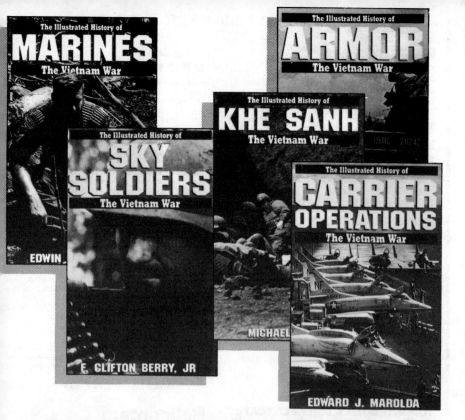

THE ILLUSTRATED
HISTORY OF
THE VIETNAM WAR

antam's Illustrated History of the ietnam War is a unique and new eries of books exploring in depth the ar that seared America to the core: war that cost 58,186 American lives, at saw great heroism and resourcefulness mixed with terrible estruction and tragedy.

The Illustrated History of the ietnam War examines exactly what appened. Every significant aspect—he physical details, the operations, and the strategies behind them—is analyzed in short, crisply written original books by established historians and journalists.

Some books are devoted to key battles and campaigns, others unfold the stories of elite groups and fighting units, while others focus on the role of specific weapons and tactics.

Each volume is totally original and is richly illustrated with photographs, line drawings, and maps.